Horizon

SPRING, 1968 · VOLUME X, NUMBER 2

Flower People Then and Now

To shed light on the subject of hippies, in this issue of Horizon several of our authors draw parallels with reformist and utopian movements of the past. For Arnold Toynbee the hippies are reminiscent of the early Christians; for J. H. Plumb, of the medieval utopian groups like the Ranters and the Brethren of the Free Spirit. The hippies themselves feel akin to the American Indians and, equally, to the mystics of India. Timothy Leary, the first guru of psychedelia, seems to remind himself of Buddha.

Our readers can hardly fail to be struck by another resemblance—that between the Flower People of San Francisco and the Flower People of Renaissance Florence who appear in Sandro Botticelli's *Primavera* (see pages 92–105). Compare, for one, Don Snyder's photograph of the bride in a hippie wedding with the face of Botticelli's Flora, which can be seen on our cover (and below.) The resemblance between Snyder's hippies and Botticelli's mythic deities is perhaps not entirely a visual accident. Many of the models who posed for Botticelli were the children of the Florentine nobility, who preferred a life of graceful dalliance to the pursuits of banking and warfare by which their fathers lived.

Those who feel that the hippies may have a brutal shock coming to them can also find support in the history of Florence. For the society that felt an affinity with Botticelli's painting was brought up short by the thunderclap of Savonarola (see pages 106–111). One of those affected by his prophecies of doom was the artist himself, who, legend says, threw some of his own nude paintings into the Friar's bonfire of "vanities."

Another article in this issue that has relevance to the hippie movement is Arthur Koestler's brilliant but also frightening essay about the human

Hippie bride

Botticelli's Flora

Horizon is published every three months by American Heritage Publishing Co., Inc.

PRESIDENT
James Parton

EDITORIAL COMMITTEE
Joseph J. Thorndike, *Chairman*
Oliver Jensen
Richard M. Ketchum

SENIOR ART DIRECTOR
Irwin Glusker

SENIOR EDITOR, HORIZON
Marshall B. Davidson

PUBLISHER, HORIZON
Paul Gottlieb

Editorial and executive offices:
551 Fifth Avenue, New York, N.Y. 10017.

EDITOR
Joseph J. Thorndike
MANAGING EDITOR: Charles L. Mee, Jr.
ARTICLES EDITOR: Robert Cowley   ART EDITOR: Jane Wilson
ART DIRECTOR: Kenneth Munowitz
ASSOCIATE EDITORS: Shirley Tomkievicz, Barbara Klaw
CONTRIBUTING EDITOR: Walter Karp
ASSISTANT EDITORS: Alice D. Watson, Charles Folds
COPY EDITOR: Mary Ann Pfeiffer   *Assistant:* Carol R. Angell

ADVISORY BOARD: Gilbert Highet, *Chairman*, Frederick Burkhardt,
William Harlan Hale, John Walker
EUROPEAN CONSULTING EDITOR: J. H. Plumb, *Christ's College, Cambridge*
EUROPEAN BUREAU: Gertrudis Feliu, *Chief, 11 rue du Bouloi, Paris 1er*

ᴴHORIZON

A Magazine of the Arts

SPRING, 1968 · VOLUME X, NUMBER 2

mind, which appears on pages 34–43. Man, as Mr. Koestler sees him, is the victim of a fearful evolutionary mistake for which the only cure may lie in drugs. Mr. Koestler argues for a careful, scientific approach to this promised salvation. But the hippies have already plunged into the casual, indiscriminate use of a whole range of drugs, from the apparently gentle marijuana, through the clearly dangerous LSD, to the deadly methedrine, or "speed." They have been ill-served by their gurus, like Leary, who fail to draw for them the clear lines of danger.

The trouble with revolutions is that they get out of hand and, as Edmund Stillman points out (pages 28–30), often bring on violent reaction. The fabric of civilization is a pretty thin skin drawn over a mass of animal instincts. Tear that skin and the furies let out may destroy the rebels along with the old order they rebelled against.

By dropping out of our society the hippies have turned a glaring light on some of society's defects. It may be that some of them would indeed like to bring that society down, as the early Christians brought down Rome. But those of their contemporaries who would change our world, rather than destroy it, must realize that dropouts are not agents of reform. If the younger generation wants a better world, they will have to build it.   J.J.T.

All correspondence about subscriptions should be addressed to: HORIZON Subscription Office, 379 West Center St., Marion, Ohio 43302.

Single Copies: $ 5.00
Subscriptions: $16.00 per year in the U.S. & Canada; elsewhere, $17.00

Annual indexes for Volumes I–IX are available at $1 each. A cumulative index for Volumes I–V is available at $3. HORIZON is also indexed in the *Readers Guide to Periodical Literature.*

The editors welcome contributions but can assume no responsibility for unsolicited material.

Title registered U.S. Patent Office

Second-class postage paid at New York, N.Y., and at additional mailing offices.

COVER: This lovely young face surrounded by flowers belongs to Flora, goddess of spring, from Botticelli's *Primavera*. One of the easiest paintings to like, it has always been one of the hardest to understand. Scholars have long tried to explain its abstruse allegory. Lately some progress in interpreting the meaning of the masterpiece has been made. The evidence is weighed in an article beginning on page 92.

The Hippies

An inquiry into the roots and meaning of youthful disaffection

The Greek portico in the picture at right was built for a railroad magnate's house in San Francisco. When the house burned down in the fire of 1906, the portico was moved to Golden Gate Park where it now stands, memorializing both the ancient Greek taste that inspired it and the nineteenth-century industrial fortune that paid for it. Ranged upon the steps of this stranded temple of Western civilization are its newest and gaudiest denizens: the hippies. Among their regalia may be seen some of the favorite symbols of their cult: flowers and beads, sandals and boots, beards and Bob Dylan hairdos, an American Indian leather dress (beneath the golden circle of "peace") and *Indian* Indian shawls to symbolize the rejection of Western values for the mystical spirit of the East. Every afternoon at about four o'clock Richard Webster, the guru with the headband, plays his brass gongs on the portico steps, and the others gather around to listen. They were photographed by Don Snyder, who is himself a pioneer in psychedelic light shows, and who made the trip from New York's East Village to San Francisco's Haight-Ashbury to record the hippies for HORIZON. Because he is one of their own, he was able to win their confidence and to show them, in

PHOTOGRAPHED FOR HORIZON BY DON SNYDER

these remarkable photographs, as they look to themselves.

The hippies' credo, echoing Socrates, is "Do your thing." Very well. HORIZON's thing is the study of our own civilization in the long view of history. In this issue we have asked several historians to consider what roots the hippies may have in the past and what meaning they may hold for the future. Our authors disagree on some things, but they all accept the hippies as a phenomenon that society will ignore or laugh off or try to suppress at its peril.

Perhaps the first thing to realize about the hippies is that they are not an isolated band of juvenile misfits. If they are a lunatic fringe, they are the fringe of a largely invisible movement a hundred times the size of their own very visible cult. This movement has grown up on every college campus in the country and has opened a gap between the generations wider than any that Scott Fitzgerald ever thought of. The hippie cult itself, with its beards and drugs and outlandish clothes, may soon flower and die. But it will not leave our civilization unchanged. For the movement it makes so dramatic is a widespread rejection by American youth of the values by which their parents have lived.

In view of this rejection some observers think it strange that the hippies have found so much sympathy in the straight, middle-class, grown-up world. But the hippies are, for the most part, the children of the middle class, and the truth may be that they are not so much in revolt as they think they are. They have at least learned a lesson from their parents: that the pursuit of a life of material comfort and social conformity leaves grown men and women with a vague but persistent feeling of uneasiness.

Children are rarely insensitive to the dissatisfaction their parents feel, and they have learned this lesson well. Having sensed their parents' tacit rejection of a life that seems somehow hollow, the children now reject it openly—sometimes zestfully, sometimes violently, sometimes with delightful results, sometimes with tragic results. It cannot be far wrong to say that these youngsters of the middle class seek a life style that their parents wish they had sought while they still had time. They are, in that sense, fulfilling their parents' wishes—and that alone may explain why middle-aged editors pay them so much attention. When we react to them, we react to an image of ourselves. And when we judge them, we judge ourselves. ✹

ABOVE: *A hippie couple stand as sedately as two figures in a daguerreotype in front of New York's glass-and-aluminum Lever House. The young lady is a computer programmer, her escort an artist.*

OPPOSITE: *On the steps of a weather-beaten house in San Francisco, Bobby Beausoleil, leader of a rock group called The Magic Powerhouse of Oz, sports the kind of apparel that once adorned cigar-store Indians. The gingerbread house with its motto from Rabelais is home for a transient population of artists, musicians, and underground film makers.*

The Secular Heretics

Take a medieval religious sect like the Brethren of the Free Spirit.
Remove God. Add acid. Put them in California,
and what do you have? A social revolution carried out by the young
against the crumbling values of the
straight, adult world? Perhaps. But social rebels have never lasted
without a political creed and program

In late February, 1967, a stark-naked man stood near the sanctuary of the Glide Memorial Church in San Francisco; about him men and women, waving incense, chanted to the throb of the Congo drums; topless belly-dancers wove in and out; psychedelic colors flashed across the church; and time and time again the sad, humanity-haunted face of Christ was projected above the crowd. Adolescents caressed and loved by the altar or withdrew to another room provided with a plastic bed. And so it went on until the early hours of the morning, when the church elders "lost their cool" and called it a day.

In Cologne, about 1325, the Brethren of the Free Spirit met in their luxurious secret chapel. There a live Christ celebrated mass, a naked preacher exhorted the brethren to return to primeval innocence, to strip, to love; for those who had become one with God there could be no sin, no church, no property. Love and the ecstatic experience was all. The church of the pope and the kingdoms of princes were evil. Take from them all that was needed, cheat them, lie to them, for innocence and love were

At a flower wedding near San Francisco, the best man bestows a kiss on a bridal attendant. The scene is Mount Tamalpais, where the wedding and a "music be-in" were being held simultaneously.

beyond crime as well as beyond sin. The celebrants responded to the preacher and loved hard, there and then. What better place than a church for copulation that was beyond sin?

In Hampshire, in 1649, William Franklin and his soul mate and bed companion Mary Gadbury found God within themselves, gave up work, lived in voluntary poverty, rejected sin, and encouraged their little flock of Ranters to revel in obscenity, promiscuity, and drink. They were not alone —little bands of these religious "hippies" buzzed like wasps' nests throughout Cromwell's England. They were eventually stifled, not by the savage laws of the Commonwealth, but by their first cousins, the Quakers, whose early philosophy was hip with a difference. The first Quakers sometimes walked naked through the villages of Leicestershire, both to show disapproval of the accepted world of materialism and darkness and to proclaim their salvation and their purity as children of light. They, too, rejected the religious establishment as well as the differences of social status, wearing their hats in church to demonstrate the one and calling all men "thou" to prove the other. And they would not pay tithes. They went to jail. Nor would they take oaths or fight, so off to jail they went again. And although they eschewed physical love outside marriage, the love of all men and

women, whatever suffering it might bring, lay at the heart of their creed.

Much of the content of hippie philosophy has a long history in such religious heresies. Take promiscuity clothed in an aura of religiosity: this stretches back through the Ranters and the Free Brethren and the Spiritual Libertines and almost to Adam himself. The hippies, ignorant of history, are but a part of a chain stretching back into the Middle Ages and beyond. Why do these philosophies, heresies, call them what you will, recur so frequently in Western society? And is the present-day hippie world illumined by the light of the past?

The hippies are secular heretics, for they reject the moral principles of society, claiming to return to a purer, less hypocritical morality. What this new secular heresy has in common with religious heresies of the past, to which it possesses so many resemblances, is that it has occurred in a very affluent society. The Brethren of the Free Spirit, who were so like the hippies, flourished in the prosperous towns of Flanders and the Rhine, where society and the church had grown materialistic, given to wanton luxury and guilt-free extravagance. Also, as now, it was a time of war and of social dislocation. And the same conditions prevailed in England in the days of the Ranters and early Quakers. The philosophy of the mar-

By J. H. PLUMB

The English Ranters practiced free love, nudity, and pipe smoking, as shown in a 1650 woodcut published by a "late fellow-Ranter."

ket place had spread like bindweed over ancient morality and stifled it; political and social anarchy, with turbulence and riot, combined with seemingly meaningless civil war, gave a loathsome luminosity to the material world in the eyes of the Ranters and Quakers. Better get right out of it and dwell with the brethren, led by the inner light.

Such antipathy to the material world and to the world of government, order, discipline, and force goes deeper than heresy, however. It is a constant theme in most religions. Sometimes the church has contained it and been revivified by it. Think of Saint Francis, the son of a prosperous merchant, who divested himself of all material things and treated all that lived—birds and beasts and insects— as aspects of God. He pursued poverty like a lover and preferred the broken, the tormented, the simple, and the foolish. A hippie-saint if ever there was one. He and his followers battened on the conscience of the material world that they despised—taking the food, the alms, the shelter, as the hippies do in Haight-Ashbury. Indeed, some founders of religion seem uncomfortably close to the hippies. Beyond Saint Francis looms a larger, more formidable figure, who amid the vast riches and stupendous power of the Roman Empire had no use for it,

nor for riches, nor for strife, nor for hypocrisy; who preferred a prostitute to a prude. In the West religion that is intense, personal, and deeply felt has always been at odds with the world it has to live in.

Yet no matter how closely one compares this new secular heresy—with its total rejection of the principles and morality of the middle-class establishment—to the religious heresies and movements of the past, or indeed sees it as a part of the cycle of rejection of the materialism that has been a constant factor in Western life and thought, there remain very important differences. The hippie world is compounded not only of social heresy but of acid. Here, surely, is the break with the past.

Drugs date back at least to the neolithic revolution, when men first discovered wine and beer; both were given sacred and ritualistic functions, which they have maintained. This is true of all communities, primitive and advanced, communist or capitalist. Almost the whole of humanity has been sodden, at some time or another, with alcohol. And its use is deeply embedded in social rituals. Billions of gallons of wine, spirits, and beer are needed to sustain the social conventions of group activity. Minor drugs and narcotics, after much initial opposition, also secured social acceptance

and became a part of the social ritual. After all, James I of England hated tobacco as much as Harry Anslinger hates hemp, and coffeehouses were thought by Charles II to be dens of decadence and political treachery; but the public craving would not be denied.

Artists, particularly from the nineteenth century onward, sought powerful hallucinations through drugs. Opium, laudanum, ether, and hashish became popular in bohemian and artistic circles in nineteenth-century Europe, a process that reached its zenith in Rimbaud, who deliberately attempted a *dérèglement de tous les sens* and wrote psychedelically of the colors of vowels. But this experimentation was a means to art—an attempt to heighten consciousness for art's sake—not a way of life.

In the hippies, therefore, two historical strands have intertwined in an odd way—social heresy and the artist's quest for heightened perception through drugs. The need for the latter is, of course, due to the absence of God. Ecstasy and elation could be achieved by the mystical heretic through ritual, fasting, contemplation, or flagellation, as long as they were intensified by a sense of God within and without. For the hippie, God scarcely exists, having been replaced by a vague sense of the oneness of humanity that is quite insufficient to create the heightened consciousness needed for hallucinations or ecstatic experience.

The hippies' ancestry, however, is European rather than American, which, perhaps, is one of the reasons why their impact in America has been so shocking. During the nineteenth century the American artist occasionally toyed with decadence or drugs, but, like Poe, he was an oddity. There were no Coleridges, no Baudelaires, no Rimbauds, no Verlaines, no Wildes, not even a Byron or a Shelley. In America the need to fly from materialism, from the grossness of a conscious world, was assuaged by the

West, either actively or imaginatively. Nature, wild and untamed, was there in abundance to soothe a Thoreau or to ease a Parkman. Nothing was easier in nineteenth-century America than to contract out of urban, commercial civilization. Now it is impossible, as it has been in Europe for many centuries. Not because there are not enough ponds for putative Thoreaus or Oregon Trails for embryonic Parkmans, but because myth has grown feebler; myths can only be sustained and given meaning by the needs of society. This aspect of American life —half dream, half reality—has lost its social dynamic. Pioneer America is meaningless not only to hippies but to the nation at large. It has been commercialized into package tours down the Grand Canyon or up the Santa Fe Trail. Escape is easier within oneself. Indeed, there is nowhere else to go.

Furthermore, America is beginning to be afflicted with those ills that beset Italian and Flemish towns of the late Middle Ages—a contraction of opportunity for their middle class or their artisan young. Medieval heretics were often drawn, as were the early Quakers, from the class of skilled artisans in times of depression and economic contraction or in periods of rapid social and technological change that proved inimical to their crafts. The hippies are largely the waste products of extensive university education systems; they are the dropouts who are creatively or intellectually unsuited to the intense competitive system of a Horatio Alger America. The acceptance of failure and the withdrawal from society are deeply satisfying solutions to anxiety—especially if there is the ultimate safety net of middle-class parents. Religious heresy was rare among the abject poor: they preferred saints and miracles. And hippies are not common in the black ghettos of America.

And therein lies a danger; for although individuals and groups can opt out of the political and moral structures of society, the majority of the nation cannot. And opting out changes nothing but the individual. No religious heresy of total or partial withdrawal from society has changed a nation for better or worse. Advancement in social and political justice can only come through political action, revolution, or civil war, as indeed the history of America demonstrates. If the hippies develop a philosophy of active civil disobedience, the picture may change. If they do not, there will be enormous *political* danger in the growth of hippiedom. The aesthetes and decadents, as well as many sensitive liberals, withdrew likewise from active politics in the Germany of the twenties and early thirties. Politics for them were corrupt, violent, and dishonest; withdrawal seemed to possess a higher morality, to be a more sensitive reaction. A withdrawal of a large segment of the younger generation of the middle class from participation in politics may easily lead, as it did in Germany, to a situation ripe for totalitarian politics. One of the most disquieting aspects of the hippie world is the cultivation of the American Indian and the turning away from the Negro and his problems—which create the central crisis of American politics. Lucy may be in the Sky with Diamonds but it is the Negro in the ghetto who matters.

But will this secular heresy grow? After all, medieval heresies rarely lasted. They were quickly rendered ineffective if not obliterated. They were sporadic fires that only ravaged briefly the healthy body of the church. And even the Ranters were quietly absorbed by the Quakers, who disciplined themselves to live alongside, if not within, the society they despised. Other, less ecstatic and more socially oriented heresies, however, such as those that occurred at the Reformation, established themselves successfully. Printing in the fifteenth century broke down the localization of medieval heresy; social dislocation and economic change in the sixteenth century gave new heresies opportunities for growth and victory denied to heresy in the Middle Ages.

Indeed, the potential for the growth of heresy is in direct proportion to the means of communication that are available. At the present time secular heresy has an even greater communications system at its command than that enjoyed by Luther and his allies. Hippies are news, to be exploited by all means of modern communication —press, radio, television, and films. Hence their message and their way of life spread like a virus, leaping from state to state, from country to country, from continent to continent, in the briefest possible time. And they provide by their dress, their buttons, their posters, paint, and pot, quick bucks for the commercially adroit. The consumer society they hate fertilizes their growth. And like the great religious heresies of the Reformation, which succeeded in establishing themselves as orthodoxies, this new secular heresy has begun to spread internationally in a way the beats never did; nor for that matter did the London teddy boys or the mods or rockers. Groups of hippies have emerged in London, in Cambridge, in Oxford, even in the provincial towns of England. Leicester has its flower people, and its park has witnessed its first love-in. The Provos in Holland will soon be riding their white bicycles with tulips in their hair and bells on their handle bars. Already there are feeble attempts—and they will grow stronger—to give these seemingly spontaneous growths international organization and common propaganda.

The success of any religious or secular heresy requires a social context that will nurture and strengthen it. In return it must meet the aspirations of and create the opportunities for not merely a handful of folk but considerable and diverse sections of a community. This was true for Christianity, for Lutheranism, for Calvinism, for the Quakers, Unitarians, Mormons, Methodists, and the rest, all of which began as heresies. It is as true of intellectual heresy as it is of religious. Is there a resonance between the hippies and new situations in our society that may echo louder and clearer in the near future? Maybe. Youth has achieved a freedom and an affluence that in previous societies were limited to the aristocracy and to very small sections of the rich middle class. What was once the privilege of a narrow segment of society has acquired a mass basis. Throughout history, youth—especially its elite in intelligence and creativity—has rarely been drawn to the adult world, but it has been forced to accept it and to obey it. The weight of society was too great, the structure of family life too firm, and the acceptance of the Christian morality of the churches too widespread for rebellion and rejection on the part of more than a few gifted individuals clustered in small groups. Most children and adolescents accepted, worked, obeyed, and joined the adults. Those days may be over.

The opportunity for youth to rebel successfully is made easier because society itself is no longer sure of either its institutions or its morality. After all, both were derived from a largely agrarian and craft-based society. The unitary family proved a remarkably viable basic unit in preindustrial society, and so did the extended family in the Orient. In the early stages of industrialization the family proved adequate, though far weaker; but it may be doubted if it will survive into a world molded by technology and science. Certainly its sanctions are crumbling at every level. Few fathers today possess a tenth of the authority of their grandfathers, either over workers or children, and the father is the core of the family as we know it. To the sensitive young the social structure of the adult world must seem hypocritical and luminous with decay, as ripe for revolution as the czardom of Nicholas II. And I suspect that this attitude is acquiring the force of truth in Moscow as well as New York. Because social institutions have

lasted ten thousand years does not mean that they are eternal: ten thousand years is a very brief span in the history of mankind.

The family as an institution may have reached a danger point, just as the aristocracy did in 1789 or the Roman Catholic Church at the time of the Reformation. The situations, oddly enough, are not dissimilar. Institutions that are unsure of themselves, given to practices that do not agree with their avowed ideals, often crumble before a sharp radical attack, as long as this attack has a wide base. And this is the current situation between youth and its social targets in the adult world—marriage, monogamy, family life. It may not be too farfetched to conceive of the Western world being caught up in a new type of social upheaval: a social-revolutionary young attacking the institutions not of political life but of adult living. Possible, but, I think, unlikely.

For the hippies do not possess the most important weapon in all revolutionary movements—a coherent ideology that interlocks belief and action, that combines philosophy with the strategy and tactics of action. If one looks back at the successful historical movements or the triumphant political and social revolutions of the past, one sees that they have always possessed a strong intellectual content as well as deep emotional drives. An active ideology—coherent, rational within its own principles—marks Calvinism as well as communism, the Quakers as well as the Jacobins. But the hippie world is a flight from the intellect and all that the intellect implies. It does not wish to dominate reality but to flee from it: to mock the adult world, not capture and change it. It possesses attitudes but not an ideology.

The hippie movement relates most closely to those ecstatic heresies of the Middle Ages that were also savagely anticlerical, that dwelt with bitterness on the riches, the greed, the corruption, of the clergy as opposed to the simplicity and poverty of Christ: the

The Grateful Dead, one of psychedelia's leading "acid-rock" singing groups, are arrayed, opposite, near Morning Star. They are Phil Lesh, Bob Weir, Pig Pen, Jerry Garcia, and Bill the Drummer.

contrast between the reality and the ideal. In this, the hippies' criticism by implication and by action of the straight world—its self-indulgence, its hypocrisy, its materialism—may lie their greatest contribution to society. The alarming gulf between avowed intention and action—as in Vietnam—is leading to moral bankruptcy. The American dream, like America's manifest destiny, is dissolving, giving way to a future not of hope but of nightmare. If the hippies force us to look at ourselves morally and spiritually naked, then well and good; but they may provoke a blinder and less sensitive reaction. They are playing as dangerously with social passions as any heretic played with religious passions in the Middle Ages. And remember how society turned on *them*, how its inquisitors rooted them out, tortured them, burned them, extirpated their women and children, purged society of its danger. America, faced by insoluble problems, made frantic by riot and by the prospect of moral defeat, may vent its spleen and crush all liberal attitudes, using as one of its excuses the social nonconformity of the hippies. Heresies without ideology or the discipline necessary for political action have usually ended in disaster.

The hippies are a part of a social and historical process, and many strands are united in their beliefs and actions; but so far in man's long history no movement that has ignored power has ever succeeded, and all groups who have made a cult of social anarchy have either been defeated or destroyed. In the absence of a political creed and of a program the hippies must be regarded as a symptom, not a social force—they are a living phantom bred by the decadent hypocrisy of so much of America's social and political morality.

Doing Their Thing at Morning Star

From New Harmony on, the lesson has always been the same: America is hard on utopias

I have become a Harmonite and mean to spend the remainder of my days in this abode of peace and quietness... I am at length free—*my body is at my own command, and I enjoy mental liberty, after having long been deprived of it.*

—WILLIAM PELHAM, LETTER
FROM NEW HARMONY, *1825*

Why do I live at Morning Star? I groove here. I feel myself at peace. I feel empathy.

—A RESIDENT OF MORNING STAR, *1967*

Within a half-hour after I had walked up a steep hill and through a grove of redwoods into the Morning Star Ranch, a rural commune of hippies north of San Francisco, I found myself stripped down to my shorts, attempting to hold a Yoga position called the Thunderbolt. There were six of us in the hillside clearing: Sandy, a Negro who had been protesting that he wanted no part of Yoga and was now complaining that it had given him a Charley horse; a young Mexican-American who was already quite expert; an army veteran with his name tattooed on his shoulder; a boy I shall call Milt, who, with his ragged black beard, his mop of long frizzly hair, and his thick glasses mended with adhesive tape, looked the epitome of the hippie; myself, white of skin and stiff of muscle; and Lou Gottlieb, a reformed forty-four-year-old folk singer and musicologist as well as the owner of the Morning Star property and the spiritual and temporal leader of the community.

"Man, that bumblebee's bothering me," Sandy said, swatting at an insect that was hovering over his back.

"Leave him alone, he's just trying to make friends," Gottlieb said. "You're probably the first spook he's ever seen."

Sandy grunted and tried an exercise called the Cobra, while Gottlieb exhorted us to stretch our necks backward until we could feel the flash of enlightenment that is said to come to the adept. While the rest of us were straining, Sandy suddenly stood up and, pulling on his clothes, announced "I got to call my wife."

"You have to do *what?*" Gottlieb demanded.

"Call my wife, man."

Gottlieb laughed.

"I mean it," Sandy said desperately. "I got to call the old lady."

Gottlieb laughed again, and Sandy loped off into the trees, presumably heading toward the glass-and-aluminum pay booth that stands like a relic of a departed alien civilization in the midst of the shacks and wigwams of Morning Star. Gottlieb instructed us to lay ourselves out in a position called the Corpse and count our breathing to fifty. When I finished and sat up, he was striding away toward the woods, a tall, dark, rather gaunt man with an authoritative manner and a full black beard like a prophet's.

After we had put on our clothes, the veteran bummed a cigarette from me, pinched out some of the tobacco at the end, and mixed a "cocktail," using the cigarette and the remains of a joint of marijuana that he produced from his pocket. Milt, the bearded one, told me he had recently found Yoga a great comfort while he was doing five days in the county jail. When I asked what he had been arrested for, he said that he had been caught stealing $1.26 worth of food in a chain grocery.

"You really got to do this Yoga every day," the Mexican-American boy told me.

Most of those who come to look at us seem highly pleased, but they see only the outside.

—THOMAS PEARS, LETTER
FROM NEW HARMONY, 1826

I don't believe in nudism myself; I'd be uncomfortable. And I think everyone should be clothed at the dinner table.

—LOU GOTTLIEB, 1967

Apart from certain details of style (drugs, primarily), the thirty or more rural communes that have sprung up over the country during the past year or so call strongly to mind the classic American utopias that flourished during the last century. Utopias were then, as they are becoming now, a considerable movement; writing in 1870, John Humphrey Noyes, the historian of early American socialism, counted forty-seven colonies that had already come and gone, a list that ran from the Alphadelphia Phalanx to the Peace Union settlement.

The great majority of these utopias, to be sure, consisted of farming colonies of pious German immigrants such as made up the Shaker and the Rappist groups, drawn together by a common regard for the virtues of hard work and the more radical forms of evangelical Christianity. Other roads to salvation, however, were sought by the colonists at Brook Farm (Massachusetts), the Oneida community (New York), and New Harmony (Indiana). Parallels that bridge a century and a half are not hard to find between these older colonies and the new. The transcendental world view of Brook Farm, the free love at Oneida, the constant dissonance between the ideal and the practical at New Harmony, are all echoed to some extent at such latter-day utopias as Timothy Leary's Millbrook colony

By KENNETH LAMOTT

Lou Gottlieb, founding father of Morning Star, stands among the sunflowers of his utopia

in rural New York; Drop City, which is a village of geodesic domes built from junk automobile tops near Trinidad, Colorado; the Tolstoy colony near Davenport, Washington; and, of course, Morning Star itself.

Morning Star, in fact, lies within a few miles of the sites of three utopian communes that flourished in the latter part of the nineteenth century. (The longest-lived of these was the Brotherhood of the New Life, founded by the mystic and poet Thomas Lake Harris at Fountain Grove, California, in 1875. It lasted as a utopia until 1892 but survived as a commercial vineyard for forty-two years more.) The guiding principles of Morning Star are not easy to classify, but if I were to try, I should describe its operative principles as an amalgam of primitive Christianity, Zen, Yoga, social nud-

ism, and philosophical anarchism.

"Everybody's free to do his own thing," I was told by a red-bearded man I found sitting in the sun on the porch of what is called the Upper House. "Everybody's welcome here, everybody who wants to get away from that Great Society down there. Lou has only one strict rule: no campfires. I guess there are about sixty or seventy people here during the week and twice that on weekends. If you want to work, you can. If you don't want to, you don't have to. As I say, everybody's free to do his own thing.

The climate here is warm and easy in the summer, without a drop of rain falling from June to September. In the apple orchard and among the redwood groves that cover Morning Star's thirty-one acres, mobile youngsters from San Francisco and

New York and Vancouver and Louisville and Chicago have erected their pads, which range from conventional campers' tents and solid wooden huts to tepees and brushwood hogans. One resident was discovered in a hollowed-out redwood stump, which he had equipped with a flat roof. He was chewing redwood bark: he said it gave him a feeling of closeness to his home. Another settler is building a substantial three-room house. Many of the pads are decorated with the iconography of the 1960's—the nuclear disarmament symbol, LOVE, and "god's eyes" of brightly colored yarn —but there are also a couple of life-sized crosses and a sign with the legend JESUS IS THE WAY.

In the winter it rains often, and the nights grow cold to the freezing point, but on a pleasant summer's day

15

For New Harmony Robert Owen planned a vast quadrangular city walled by public buildings and peak-roofed houses. In reality it was built like any other Indiana town.

it is not hard to become convinced that this *is* the great good place, the New Jerusalem. The charm is so powerful that even Paul Stefani, a narcotics investigator in the local district attorney's office, confessed after his first visit that "I came back to the office and kidded the guys that I wouldn't be around much longer, that I was going to defect."

For the weekend tourists there is at least one clear attraction. Casual nudism is endemic, and on a Sunday ranchers in sombreros, the local gentry in golf caps, and high-school boys in crew cuts stalk the hills and groves with their Polaroids. They don't have to look far, for the whole point of going around naked, of course, is to celebrate the innocent glory of the flesh. For what it is worth, let me add the observation that nudism at Morning Star, as elsewhere, seems generally antierotic in tendency, with none of the nuzzling, groping, and covert probing that goes on in every corner of the best-regulated beach.

I am come to this country to introduce an entire new state of society; to change it from an ignorant, selfish system to an enlightened social system which shall gradually unite all interests into one, and remove all causes for contests between individuals.

—ROBERT OWEN, FOUNDER OF NEW HARMONY, 1825

We are running a pilot study in survival. The hippies are the first wave of the

technological unemployed. Continuing the tradition of the intentional community—Brook Farm, Oneida, New Harmony—the problem is to get a piece of land and see who it attracts. We are attempting a definition of a style of life.

—LOU GOTTLIEB, FOUNDER OF MORNING STAR, 1967

New Harmony, which lasted from 1825 to 1830, was founded by Robert Owen, a self-made English textile magnate who sank some two hundred thousand dollars into his unsuccessful socialist experiment on the banks of the Wabash but who is remembered chiefly as a pioneer of the British Labor movement. Lou Gottlieb, the founder and patron of Morning Star, is as diverse in his interests as Owen, although in a considerably different style. The last time I'd seen Gottlieb had been many years ago at the San Francisco night club called the hungry i, where he had been plucking a double bass with the Gateway Singers and singing urban folk songs of his own composition. (One of these, as I recall, began, "Oh, Doctor Freud, oh Doctor Freud,/ How I wish you had been differently employed. . . .") Since then he has led another trio called the Limeliters, while earning a Ph.D. in musicology at Berkeley.

In the late spring of 1966 he moved out to Morning Star. As the word spread that settlers were welcome, other people joined him, including some Diggers—members of the internal Salvation Army of the

hippie movement, which feeds the mind-blown hungry and clothes the naked. Although Morning Star has been identified as a Digger community, this was never strictly true. Some food grown at Morning Star went to Haight-Ashbury by way of the Diggers, but the alliance was in the nature of things a loose one.

When I first walked up the hill into Morning Star, I was met by the sound of a Mozart sonata being played by a performer of obviously professional caliber. It was Gottlieb, of course, practicing in his cabin, which is just large enough for a piano, a bed, some books, and Gottlieb himself. I later discovered he practiced six or seven hours a day, for a concert debut to take place when he turns fifty, he said. Not wanting to disturb him, I walked on up to the Upper House, where I was shortly to be recruited for the Yoga session, and it wasn't until well into the afternoon that I returned to the cabin.

The daily regime at Morning Star is hard to describe in any convincing detail, for its pure and literal anarchy outrages all one's middle-class bias in favor of order and organization. The style of life here has pushed permissiveness to its outer limits. Work does manage to get done—meals are cooked, dishes are washed, the tomatoes, cabbages, pumpkins, and beans in the garden somehow get tended— but nobody has been assigned to any particular duty. People sleep, talk, smoke pot, talk, lie in the sun, talk, meditate, talk, sing, and talk.

In the afternoon, I joined six or seven other people, both hippie and straight, who had gathered outside Gottlieb's cabin to listen to him practice. I fell into conversation with a San Franciscan named Karl, whom I guessed to be in his seventies—a short, compact man in golden corduroys, who wore his hair and beard in the classic style of Buffalo Bill Cody. He told me that although he doesn't live at Morning Star he comes up on weekends to refresh his spirit. Among the others were a pleasant, round-faced Negro boy and a spare, deeply tanned man whom I had already noticed several times because he had a habit of keeping his face, eyes closed, lifted directly into the sun.

There was also a pretty college-age girl I shall call Karen, who had come up with a bearded boy to visit Morning Star for the day. They were both holding flowers and looking a little self-conscious. Karen burbled on and on, while Karl patiently and courteously fielded her observations that it was all so wonderful that it was hard to believe, that it was awfully pretty up here, that it must be a wonderful place to live, and so on and so on. Then, with a burst of Beethoven, the piano stopped, and Gottlieb came out to join us, dressed conventionally in a dark sport shirt, slacks, white athletic socks, and an old pair of loafers.

"I just want to tell you how pretty that was," Karen exclaimed. "You're a *good* piano player."

"Oh, God," Gottlieb said quietly and retreated a step.

Karen forged on remorselessly. "It's such a beautiful place I wouldn't mind living here myself. Don't you love it?"

Gottlieb, who is a highly articulate and even voluble man, disappeared silently. He returned with a paper sign that read: THIS BODY HAS ALREADY TALKED 'WAY TOO MUCH. He sat on the bench, pulled up his legs Yoga fashion, placed the sign on his lap, looked into trees, and said nothing. A black and white puppy approached. Undismayed, Karen exclaimed, "What a cute puppy! What's its name?"

"God," somebody on the other side of Gottlieb said.

"What a funny name for a puppy!" Karen cried. "Here, God! Come here, God!"

Looking rather nervously over its shoulder, the puppy departed at a fast trot. After a moment of blessed silence, Karen said, crestfallen, "Oh! I didn't realize I was being put down."

She recovered in a moment, however, and dashed off in high spirits to show a newly arrived friend around Morning Star. Looking after her, Gottlieb said mildly, "And to think that's exactly the sort of girl I used to run around after."

He closed his eyes and folded his hands in an attitude of meditation. I found a comfortable place on the deck and dozed in the warm sun with my back against the cabin. The others did likewise or wandered away. It was very pleasant.

Suddenly a car erupted on the narrow dirt road that comes up from the parking lot and ground to a dusty halt a few feet from me. A deputy sheriff was at the wheel, a young, beefy man wearing a spanking fresh khaki uniform. He put his head out of the window—dark glasses, square teeth, carefully combed wavy yellow hair—and said, "Hi, Lou."

"Hello," Gottlieb said courteously.

"Can we have a word with you?"

"Of course."

The deputy churned the car up the gravel a few extra feet toward the cabin and got out with his passenger. The second man was older, a graying crew-cut type wearing a sport shirt with the tails out and sharply pressed slacks. The bottom of a well-worn woven leather pistol holster protruded from under his shirt.

"I wonder if we could talk privately," the uniformed deputy said.

"Certainly," Gottlieb said.

I reluctantly walked away.

Now Vice and Crime no more shall stalk
  Unseen in open day,
To cross our silent, peaceful walk
  Through life's enchanting way....
                    —A NEW HARMONY SONG

If they find any evidence of organization here, I wish they would show it to me.
                    —LOU GOTTLIEB (AFTER HAVING BEEN CHARGED WITH OPERATING AN ORGANIZED CAMP IN VIOLATION OF STATE HEALTH REGULATIONS)

A tall girl who appeared to be wearing nothing except a long brown T shirt was strumming a guitar and singing to an audience of a dozen or so people in the Lower House. Some of them were sitting on a ratty sofa and a couple of overstuffed chairs. On a mattress on the floor sat a young fellow wearing a marine private's tunic and blue jeans. A thin girl in a granny dress was curled up on the other mattress. A cotton spread had been thrown over her, and a half-eaten apple lay near her mouth. Because she looked withdrawn and glassy-eyed, I assumed she was on an acid trip, but when I looked closer, she seemed merely sick and unhappy. A car had just come back from town with groceries, and out in the kitchen several people were getting dinner together.

I decided to go to the well, which occupies a strategic position between the Upper House, the Lower House, and Gottlieb's cabin. I found Milt at the well and asked him if he knew what was on the minds of the depu-

At Morning Star, commune members are shown putting up the frame of a tepee. Easy to construct, the Plains Indians' dwelling is a favorite design at many of the hippie colonies.

17

ties, still talking earnestly to Gottlieb, who looked completely undisturbed.

"Somebody in a sheriff's car comes up here about twice a week," Milt said. "Usually it's about illegal campfires or underage runaways or sanitation." Milt went on, grinning cheerfully, "The cops aren't very high on my list of worries. Not having a warm place to sleep comes first. Then comes going hungry. Cops are third."

I asked if the sheriff had ever made any trouble about drugs.

"Not yet," he said, "but we don't have any guarantee about the future. I make sure I'm never carrying any pot on me. I do my best to smoke only other people's pot. It's pretty hard for them to bust you just for smoking. Usually they have to prove possession." As far as I could tell, marijuana was smoked freely, but there was not much visible evidence of LSD use. One boy whom I asked said, "Oh hell, who wants to get on acid and go around all stinking with sweat?"

Karl, the elderly man with flowing gray hair, came up to the well to say good-bye. He was going back to the city, he said, to take a sick girl to the hospital.

I asked if this was the girl I'd seen in the Lower House.

He nodded. "I don't know if you noticed, but her face is all swollen up. She's been on speed [methedrine]. It rots out the teeth, and she's a pretty sick girl." We shook hands, and he walked over to his camper truck. The girl was already lying on a bunk in the back, and a boy got in to keep her company, shutting the door behind him.

By this time the deputies had disappeared, and a number of people had drifted back toward Gottlieb's cabin. Milt, who had taken off his clothes, which he was now holding in one hand, was telling an inquisitive tourist that he had gone to Hebrew school for six years. Gottlieb had resumed his position of meditation.

I walked through the orchard and back through the redwoods. As I came out of the woods, I stepped almost into the middle of a quiet group of two bearded men and two girls, who were sitting in the shade. None of them were wearing clothes, although the men had straw hats on. As I looked back at them, it struck me that they had fallen almost precisely into the easy postures of the picnicking bohemians in Manet's *Le Déjeuner sur l'Herbe*.

Gottlieb was looking somewhat more convivial when I returned to his cabin. A disciple was sitting at his feet, a muscular man in shorts and sandals, with long reddish hair and a beard. He was rocking back and forth on his heels, staring unblinkingly at Gottlieb and, when I stopped, at me. I thanked Gottlieb for his hospitality, and he invited me to come back; I said I thought I would.

It wasn't until I was sitting in my car that I realized I hadn't found out what the sheriff had come for this time.

Oh, if you could see some of the rough uncouth creatures here, I think you would find it rather hard to look upon them exactly in the light of brothers and sisters.

—SARAH PEARS, LETTER
FROM NEW HARMONY, 1826

It's not like it used to be. Too many outsiders have been coming up here during the summer—Hell's Angels, tourists, people who come up for the wrong reasons. I don't know if Lou's right, letting everybody in.

—A RESIDENT OF MORNING STAR, 1967

By the time I returned to Morning Star a few days later, the community had suffered an act of violence that demonstrated the impossibility of a utopia's cutting itself off entirely from the dominant pressures of the world outside. A fight had broken out one night between Negroes and whites, apparently over a white girl. Some of the Negroes had retrieved guns that they had hidden in the bushes and had fired several shots. Nobody

had been hit, but another Negro, angry and frightened, had called the cops. (It wasn't, in fact, the first incident of the sort. Earlier in the summer a crowd of Gypsy Jokers—an "outlaw" motorcycle gang—had violently dispossessed some Negro residents from their sleeping bags.)

Although the county authorities seem to have endured Morning Star with quite remarkable forbearance up to this point, the shooting crystallized the local sentiment hostile to Gottlieb. (It is not, I think, irrelevant to note that the most emotional arguments were directed against "nudity visible from the highway." Ah, America!) The district attorney announced his intention of closing the place down, and a judge enjoined Gottlieb and a hundred John Does from running an organized camp, from parading their nudity, from building campfires, and from letting the public onto the property. A safari of officials tramped up the hill from the parking lot: the sheriff and eight deputies, a half-dozen building inspectors, FBI agents, a county supervisor, the chief probation officer, a municipal court judge, and even border patrolmen looking for Canadians.

I had, as it happened, talked to two of the Canadians on the day after the gunplay. I found them lying out in the orchard, sunning themselves in the buff. "When we get back to Canada we're going to start a place like this ourselves," a boy from British Columbia told me. When I asked what the trouble was with Morning Star, a boy from Montreal who'd been living at Morning Star since early spring said, "Before the summer everything was different. Everybody turned out for Yoga, everybody worked in the vegetable fields, everybody was on the macrobiotic diet—you know, brown rice and stuff like that. Then these outsiders moved into the Upper House and began playing the record player loud and drinking and eating meat."

He bummed a cigarette from me and lay back in the sun for a few

"The Land of Cockaigne," depicted above by Pieter Bruegel in 1567, was a legendary paradise where wine bubbled up from springs and roasted pigs ran around with knives in their backs, ready for carving. Bruegel's peasants would have liked it at Morning Star.

minutes. Then he sat up and asked, "Say, have you ever heard of a place called Tolstoy?"

I said I'd heard of it but that was all.

"It's a groovy place. They don't let *everybody in*—just people who really believe in it. They've got some organization there. Everybody knows what he's supposed to be doing."

I said it sounded somewhat different from Morning Star.

"It is," he said. "It sure is." He sounded wistful.

When I walked back to the center of the community, a series of arpeggios from the cabin told me that Gottlieb had come back. A good-looking white girl and the round-faced Negro boy were sitting on the bench outside. I knew I ought to stop and talk to Gottlieb, but the questions I thought of sounded a little fatuous now ("Mr. Gottlieb, do you think Morning Star has a future?"), and besides, I didn't want to interrupt his

practicing. And besides that, I felt more than a little depressed about the whole scene already.

Whatever the immediate causes of my depression, it turned out to be fully and unhappily justified by what happened next. After some legal backing and filling, the judge who had issued the injunction gave Gottlieb four days to bring Morning Star up to the standards of an organized camp. At the end of the four days he found Gottlieb in contempt of court and fined him five hundred dollars, with an additional five hundred to be levied for every day that any guests remained on his property.

The next day a posse of deputies arrived and pointed out to Gottlieb that the fourteen young people who had insisted on staying would cost him another five hundred dollars. Gottlieb asked his friends to leave. His friends declined. Gottlieb asked the deputies to remove his friends.

The deputies declined. Gottlieb asked what he should do. The deputies suggested that he make a citizen's arrest. Reluctantly, Gottlieb went from one person to the next, asking each one to leave and, when he wouldn't, arresting him for trespass. Then the deputies put the hippies in their cars and carted them off to jail.

A couple of days later, hearing that Gottlieb was visiting each one of the 396 citizens who had signed a petition that had helped bring on the injunction ("I'm going to try to look into their hearts"), I dialed the number of the phone booth near the well. A long time went by, there was some electronic clicking, and then a recorded female voice told me that the number was no longer in service. ✴

Kenneth Lamott, a novelist and former editor of Contact *magazine, lives in California, midway between Haight-Ashbury and the fallen Morning Star.*

19

Gurus and Boo-Hoos

The drift-along hippie life purports to be inherently religious, but even among the hippies there are always a few who try harder. These are the various sages of the movement, who appoint themselves or style themselves or merely promote themselves as religious prophets and guides. They include, among others, Arthur Kleps (bottom right), founder of the largely invisible Neo-American Church, and Allen Cohen (opposite), editor of the *Oracle*. The most famous sage, however, is Dr. Timothy Leary (top right), creator of the League for Spiritual Discovery, or LSD. Leary looks upon the chemical LSD as a sacrament, and its presumed power to arouse "latent religious sensitivities" forms the wellspring of hippie religiosity: regeneration through chemico-mystical union of the self and the universe, or, more commonly, "tuning in." On a vast, rented estate at Millbrook, in the Hudson Valley, Leary's transient disciples take the sacrament and can, at times, feel their own body cells dividing.

Discovering the true self and rejecting externals formed the message of the Buddha, who thus represents to most psychedelic believers the greatest religious teacher of all. Hippie gurus, at any rate, enjoy striking Buddha-like poses. Hippie religion is absorbent, however, and Cohen's *Oracle* also recommends Tarot cards, Hopi Indian spirits, and Henry David Thoreau. ✴

Assuming the Buddha's cross-legged pose, Timothy Leary, prime apostle of psychedelic religion, sits under a tree at Millbrook, New York, where his followers gather to take LSD, explore their real selves, and float about on a ten-square-mile estate.

Rising from his rock-pile home, Arthur Kleps offers a blessing as chief "Boo-Hoo" of his own Neo-American Church. To join Kleps's church, aspiring Boo-Hoos can write away (and send $5) to Kleps or set up a ministry without writing to Kleps.

Looking like a swami, opposite, Allen Cohen edits a journal called the Oracle *from a Haight Street office draped with Indian prints. Oriental occultism, social diatribes, and* fin-de-siècle *artwork comprise Cohen's message to the psychedelic world.*

Psychedelic Art

From the psychedelic movement there has come, inevitably, psychedelic art, and like a great deal else in the movement, it contains much that is old, much that is new, and much that is borrowed—chiefly from the Orient. On its new, futuristic side the movement offers light shows that send hurtling lights and shifting colors across walls, floors, and ceilings. More daring are the multi-media shows and total "environments" where the same lights combine with aching sounds, pulsating music, scenes from old movies, and other sensual effects that assault the human brain-circuits and, the artists hope, "vaporize the mind."

Psychedelic artists who work with light are sometimes termed lumia artists, a phrase that sounds like an ominous coinage from one of Aldous Huxley's electrochemical utopias. Psychedelic painting, on the other hand, has little of this futuristic verve. In the main it is curiously old-fashioned. The typical psychedelic painter is none other than the old landscape artist brought up to date. His intentions are similar, though the landscapes he paints are different. What a psychedelic artist tries to represent is the intense, ecstatic superdream in supertechnicolor that he has undergone through the use of a hallucinogenic drug—the inner landscape of the deeper self. Some psychedelic painters combine such "realism" with mystical symbols like the Tibetan mandala at top right and other Oriental paraphernalia. The works of art on this page and the following two pages are taken from the first authoritative book on the subject, *Psychedelic Art*, by Robert E. L. Masters and Jean Houston. ✤

Opposite, a lattice of light plays across a girl's face, in a light show produced by Jacques Kaszmacher. Such shows try to give viewers a drugless hallucinogenic trip.

The phantasmagoria above, serenely contained within a circle in a square, is the work of psychedelic painter Allen Atwell. The form is based on a Tibetan symbol known as a mandala. It appears below in a "painting in lights" entitled Lotus Mandala, *by a communal group of psychedelic artists, the USCO ("Us Company") of Garnerville, N.Y.*

BOTH: FROM *Psychedelic Art*, PRODUCED BY MARSHALL LEE; A BALANCE HOUSE BOOK, GROVE PRESS, N.Y., 1968

Allen Atwell

A Psychedelic Temple

The hot molten fantasia at right represents one of the high points of the psychedelic art movement. Splayed over the walls, ceiling, and floor of a New York City apartment, it comes close to achieving the professed aim of psychedelic art: "to re-create, introduce, stimulate or convey the nature or essence of the psychedelic experience." Visitors feel rather giddy in finding their way to the doorway in the center of the room or to the staircase, hung with a man's coat at lower right.

Described as a "psychedelic temple," this is the work of Allen Atwell, whose mandala painting appears on the preceding page. A former associate professor of art at Cornell, Atwell at forty-two is a well-trained artist, and unlike so many instant converts to Orientalism, he has spent several years—some of the time as a Fulbright scholar—living and studying in India and Southeast Asia. His psychedelic temple, or environmental painting, breaks with the long modern tradition of easel painting. By creating a setting instead of adorning a wall, Atwell and other environmental painters have returned to an older tradition that Michelangelo, perhaps, might still recognize despite the psychedelic guise.

24

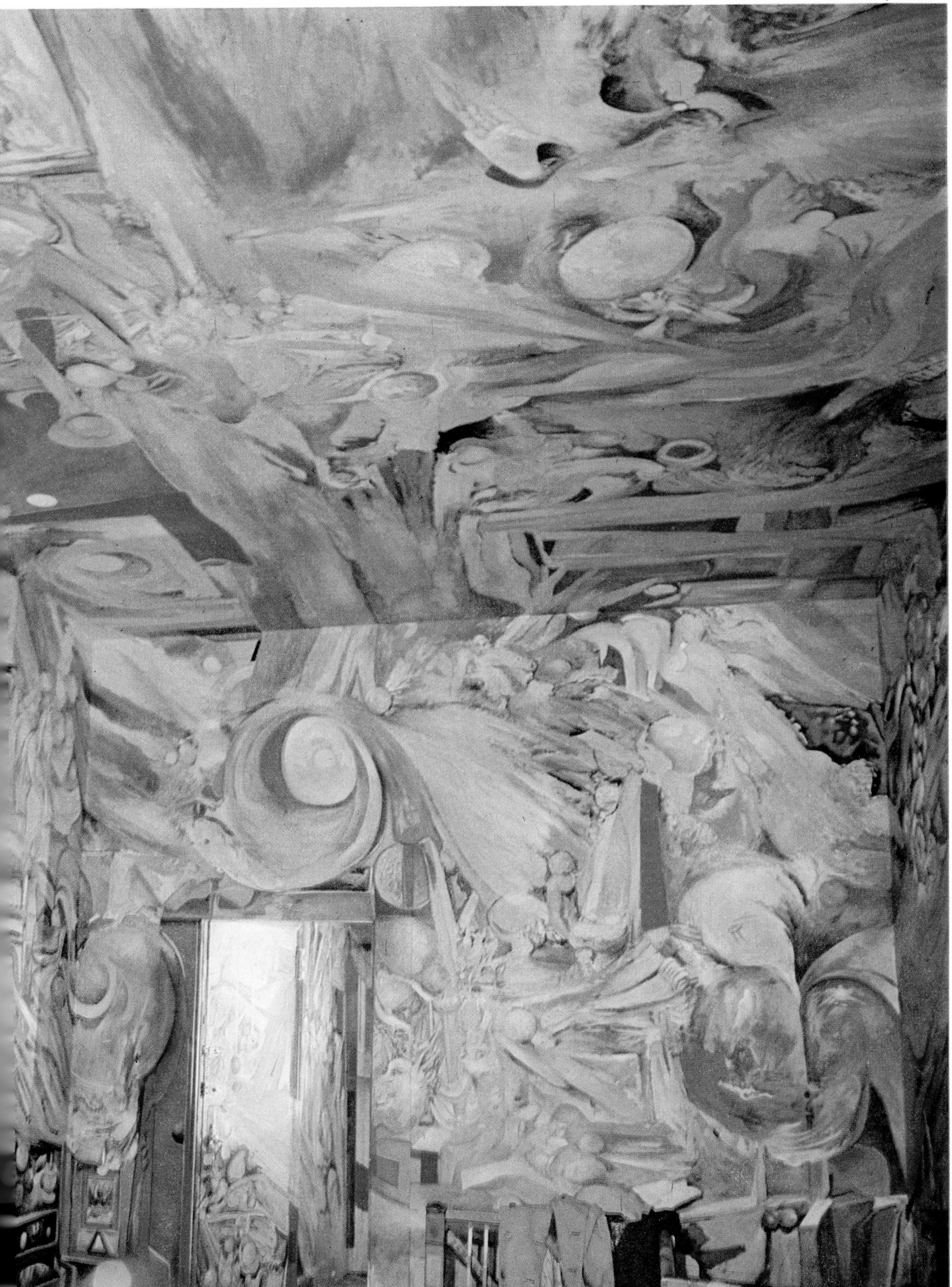

As It Was in Rome...

Few could imagine, in the second century, what the early Christians would do to the ancient world

I have been visiting the United States since 1925. Before my latest visit I had been absent for two years, and I came away with the impression that in these two years there has been more change in American life than in all the previous forty.

During those forty years I had been watching the so-called "American way of life" (i.e., the urban middle-class businessman's way of life) going from strength to strength. Since the Second World War the affluence that is the product and pride of this way of life had spread downward till it had come to be shared by perhaps four-fifths of the American people. It had also been promising—or threatening—to overshadow the earth. It had become the ideal and objective of underdeveloped foreign peoples —their unavowed objective if their official ideology was anticapitalist.

Today this hitherto triumphant way of life is being repudiated in the United States itself—and this in an unexpected quarter: not among the "underprivileged" (who are now also in revolt), but among the children of parents whose personal and family histories have been "success stories." This is a revolt of the affluent-born against their parents' ideal—the ideal of affluence won by working hard with the object of making money rather than for the sake of the work's intrinsic value. It is also a revolt against the power that wealth brings, and against the ruthless use of this power, in economic competition and in war, to preserve the privileges of the privileged.

The most flamboyant representatives of the insurgent generation are, of course, the hippies, but these are only the unsubmerged tenth part of the iceberg. The same spirit is latent among the hippies' quiet contemporaries who have not dropped out of high school or university and have not advertised their alienation by giving themselves an un-

conventional outward appearance. Will this rejection of the old way lead to the starting of a new way? It is still too early to guess; so, being a historian, I turn to the past for light.

In the second century of the Christian Era the Greco-Roman way of life was apparently at its zenith, and its ideals were inspiring. Rome had banned the fratricidal wars that had been the bane of city-state patriotism and had thus set her empire's Greek inhabitants free to devote their energies to the arts and sciences that were the glory of the Greek way of life. And then the Greek intellectuals and the Roman political authorities woke up to the disconcerting fact that their cherished way of life was being challenged by a rapidly growing countersociety, recruited from their own ranks, that repudiated what the Greco-Roman civilization stood for, believed that it had a manifest destiny to be "the new people," and was willing to back its beliefs by suffering martyrdom.

The early second-century correspondence between the encyclopedic man of letters Pliny and the emperor Trajan reveals the perplexity and concern that the Christians were already producing in the minds of the Roman public authorities. Since A.D. 63 the penalty for a declared and impenitent Christian had been death. Trajan's policy was to avoid the passing of death sentences whenever possible, but there were Christians who forced the government's hand by defiant demonstrations of disloyalty to the Roman state on the ground of loyalty to their own Christian god. They refused to cast a grain of incense on the altar of the goddess Rome and the god Caesar, and this was equivalent in present-day American terms to the act of a conscientious objector who burns his draft card. The Greco-Roman civilization's weak point was the inadequacy of its religion. Its god was the same god as that of today's American Establish-

ment. Its god was the state; and states are unsatisfying objects of worship, for they are not gods in truth; they are just public utilities. The Christians had a better god to offer; there was a spiritual vacuum in the Greco-Roman world, and Christianity could fill it.

Is it conceivable that the hippie movement, with its gospel of love, could build up the equivalent of what the Christian movement built up within a hundred years of its start? Well, nothing could be more surprising than Christianity's eventual success; for its start, as described in the Acts of the Apostles, must have looked psychedelic to cultivated and respectable onlookers, both Jewish and Greek. On the Day of Pentecost, when the apostles "spoke with tongues," some of the spectators thought that they were just drunk— and this at 9:00 A.M.! Moreover, the members of the infant Christian community did not earn their living. Converts who had property sold it; the community lived, from hand to mouth, on that.

Un-Roman! Un-American! ". . . your sons and your daughters shall prophesy, and your young men shall see visions . . ." "The wind bloweth where it listeth, and thou hearest the sound thereof, but canst not tell whence it cometh, and whither it goeth . . ." With our hindsight we now know how far the rushing, mighty Christian wind of change did go. The destiny of the present rising wind of change in America is unforeseeable, so Gamaliel's advice to the Sanhedrin seems to me to be good advice for present-day affluent American parents confronted by insurgent children. ". . . **let them alone: for if this counsel or this work be of men, it will come to nought: But if it be of God, ye cannot overthrow it . . .**" ☘

In a pile of junked cars two California hippies see a wasteful, materialist culture.

By ARNOLD J. TOYNBEE

A Reckoning to Come?

Beware the revolutionists. They may seem like harmless romantics,
but their movement is a flight from
reason and responsibility. Its predictable end: reaction

If history has any single lesson, it is surely that nothing involving men is a simple calculation. "No plan survives the first shock of battle," the elder von Moltke used to say, and even Lenin, the great visionary of revolution, warned that "history is more cunning than us all."

And of all human endeavors revolution may be the chanciest, not merely in outcome—that is simple success or failure—but in what comes after "success." Yesterday's radicalism fades in unaccountable ways into today's reaction, and what the revolutionaries intended to build may turn out the precise reverse.

In France, in 1789, the dream was of the goddess Reason enthroned in Notre Dame, but for nearly two years the reality was terror in the streets, to be succeeded eventually by a disguised restoration of monarchy—a monarchy, in Napoleon's conception, more efficient and daring, but in reality more vainglorious, bellicose, and callous to lives and obligation than the Bourbons had ever dared to be.

A half-century ago, on November 6, 1917, the Red Guards stormed the Winter Palace in Petrograd and began what the Bolshevik revolutionaries confidently supposed was a new era in the history of man. Two days later, with Bolshevik forces firmly in control of the city, Lenin strode into the hall of the second all-Russian congress. He stood there, as the American journalist John Reed wrote, "gripping the edge of the reading stand, letting his little winking eyes travel over the crowd . . . apparently oblivious to the

long-rolling ovation, which lasted several minutes.

"When it finished, he said simply, 'We shall now proceed to construct the Socialist order!' Again that overwhelming human roar."

What the Bolsheviks had done that day, Lenin asserted, could not be undone; reason would triumph; history would never be the same again. Yet fifty years later we now see, despite all the hope, blood, and pain, that that epochal day in a long-ago autumn was a little less epochal than the revolutionaries supposed. How could they know that the heroic age of revolution would be succeeded by the dark years of Stalin's bureaucratic terror—a politics of *un*reason; and that those dark years in turn would be succeeded by what has proved in our own time to be merely a peculiarly dull, bureaucratic illiberalism that would shame them more? If now reason comes again to Russia, it is not the old vision of reason but the reasonableness of exhausted men.

But was the outcome quite so unforeseeable? Could not the fury of the Stalinist terror have been foreseen? And after the terror, the exhaustion? This is not to tax the revolutionaries with their breach of the old commandments of morality and abstract justice; they were, in their way, ethical men, whatever they may have written and said. But had they merely looked more deeply into themselves, they might have found the clues.

What were their ultimate sensations when they stormed the rubble heap that was all that was left of the jerry-

built empire of the czars? Was it the mere triumph of reason they were hoping for, or was there a darker side to it all? Perhaps the ultimate clue lay in the vast human roar that greeted Lenin that night before the congress. Did the prospect of power tickle? Did the command of great armies not set blood pounding in the temples of the scholarly, obscure Trotsky? Was there not something nonrational, *anti*rational, magical, even, in their professed sober hopes to build a millennium? Because, whatever the Bolsheviks' verbal pretensions to scientism and reason may have been, theirs was at bottom a wild, visionary, transmundane hope: that *perfect* order, *perfect* justice, *perfect* harmony would come to prevail when even elementary reason might have told them it could not be.

I say these things not to write one more epitaph on a revolution that died long ago, nor to dismiss the importance of the Russian Revolution itself. Whatever the contemporary outcome, that revolution in its early and middle years was one of the great dramas of mankind, enlisting great passions and unleashing great nobility.

The real point is not that revolutions, like everything else in this realm of time, come to an end. The point is that the very men who make a movement, it seems, often understand its true meaning and ultimate consequences the least. And this is true not merely of *political* revolutions. It is as true of revolutions in *ideas*, in ways of feeling. For behind every political revolt there lies, at some remove, a radi-

By EDMUND STILLMAN

cal shift in intellectual and emotional attitudes toward the world. From the earlier revolution the later cataclysm ultimately derives.

This is a matter of some relevance to our time. In the Western world the political passions of the past half-century all seem spent. We seem to have exhausted the doctrinal quarrels of Marxist and anti-Marxist, clerical and anticlerical. The hysterically believing communist and fascist masses seem to have disappeared. At the level of politics an enormous apathy has descended on us all.

But in that Western world, and in America especially, we are in the midst of what may be a great attitudinal revolution, as yet inchoate, whose political effects are still distant. This attitudinal revolution, insofar as it is American, is not the widely noted "permissiveness"—the shift in the sexual mores of the young or of the middle-aged married. (The new permissiveness, if it is a phenomenon at all, is probably nothing more than a feature of the larger process of the Europeanization of America, the breaking down of the old provincial American ethic as the result of a quarter-century's close involvement with the world.)

It is something else, and it is ominous. If a single phrase will describe it, the movement is a flight from mind. Among the practitioners of the new arts, the new politics, the new mores —and their appreciative though nonpracticing audiences as well—there seems to be a growing impatience with rationality and a search for what psychologists might call pure affect, sensation without much attention to the substance that lies beneath. Thus the New Left in politics are all attitude—romantics in their cult of violence, their contempt for bureaucratic routine, their distrust of programmatic planning—and are without any clear idea of what they would like to see. (That is why the New Left will have nothing to do with the communist movement, which is seen as

painfully dated, as indeed it is.) In the arts the contemporary mood is all rejection, not merely of official society, but of the "straight" world as a whole. And if the contemporary mood is a hunger for feeling, the new drug culture is nothing else.

The trouble is not that these movements, and the people who support them, are intrinsically bad. Even *Time* recognizes that hippies by and large are gentle creatures, that "flower power" is not meant to kill.

The trouble is that when surveying the contemporary revolutionary scene, one has the unpleasant sensation of *déjà vu*. We have met it all before; and the last time around the outcome was not good.

For the trouble with the New Left is that they are not as newly minted as they think. At their most daring best they have nothing to say that an uncompromising nineteenth-century nihilist like Bakunin could not have said—"The desire to destroy is a desire to create."

We are back in Milan in 1910, and the futurists in the cafés are pelting us with manifestoes, telling us "that all forms of imitation should be held in contempt and that all forms of originality be glorified; that we should rebel against the tyranny of . . . harmony and good taste; that a clean sweep be made . . . in order to express the vortex of modern life—a life of steel, fever, pride, and speed."

We are back in Zurich in 1916, at the Cabaret Voltaire. There is not much that can startle by its newness in the contemporary American proliferation of Brillo boxes exalted to the stature of solitary aesthetic objects; of comic-strip banalities enlarged beyond life in order to confront us with our emptiness; of do-nothing machines; or of rotting offal displayed for us, hermetically sealed, in constructs of clear plastic. It is all so very old: Dada fifty years later, and in spite of all the practice we cannot even do it as well.

Dada: noise music, nonsense verse,

antiart. Duchamp paints a mustache on the *Mona Lisa* and displays as a "ready-made" art object a urinal turned topsy-turvy. Picabia designs absurd machines without function to mock technology. Schwitters makes collages of garbage picked up in the streets. Hugo Ball recites his "abstract" verse:

gadji beri bimba glandridi laula lonni cadori
gadjama gramma berida bimbala glandri galassassa laulitalomini
gadji beri bin blassa glassala laula lonni cadorsu sassala bim . . .

Even the psychedelic art of our time is not really new, though the biochemical drug technology is—witness the surrealist visions of Max Ernst and Picasso in the twenties. They have said it all: the hot colors juxtaposed with poison greens; the swirling, cryptosexual imagery.

What is new is the mass character of these movements today; for what has happened is that while coteries of alienated artists and intellectuals have been with us for a long time, there is now a mass community of alienated *non*artists and *non*intellectuals. It is as if the true artists and intellectuals were the priesthood, the perfecti of the new dispensation, and the rest of the hip and alienated mass merely cultivated the mood, the sensation, without the commitment to create. This is part of the growing divorce between consciousness and action.

Dada was a movement of a narrow European elite. In the American environment the movement has, predictably, been democratized. The futurists, the Dadaists, and the rest were mere lonely visionaries of destruction, though more than a few of these men went on to play the role of intellectual apologists for fascism and Stalinism between the wars. The movements in America are a social fact in themselves, a potential political datum. They do not merely herald the breakdown of inherited morality; as mass movements they advance the cause. And while bourgeois hypocrisy and corruption ought to go, there is the old admonitory lesson of the last time around. Futurism condemned the sterility and sham of a Europe on the eve of cataclysm; Dada was a reaction to the carnage itself. Surrealism was a movement of the postwar wasteland. But by attacking the official values, these movements did not simply clear away the lies. They helped break down the few conventions of restraint and decency that, maimed by a century of surfeit and lying and the carnage of the 1914–18 years, had managed to survive the war itself.

The story of antirationalism did not end with antiart, and the mood that Dada bespoke was not confined to a mere intellectual elite. Eventually the mood that futurism and Dada prefigured took flesh. The power and pride of futurism became Mussolini's fascism. As Dada was antiart, so Nazism became antipolitics. Conventional economic and social analyses will not serve to explain Nazism. It was no mere economic counterattack of the lower middle classes. It was no mere political prop to the I. G. Farben or Thyssen industrial empires. Nazism was a politics of unreason. Was not Auschwitz—the death machine, the place where corpses were turned out on assembly lines—the last vicious parody of Detroit's River Rouge, the last nasty laugh at the twentieth-century triumph of the machine? What a put-on of the inherited moralities— the old Protestant virtues of saving, efficiency, and speed—when at Nuremberg a defendant named Hoess could testify:

I visited Treblinka to find out how they carried out their extermination. The camp commandant at Treblinka told me that he had liquidated 80,000 in the course of half a year. . . . He used monoxide gas and I did not think that his methods were very efficient. So when I set up the extermination building at Auschwitz, I used Zyklon B, which was a crystallized prussic acid which we dropped into the death chamber from a small opening. It took from three to fif-

teen minutes to kill the people in the death chamber, depending upon climatic conditions. . . . Another improvement we made over Treblinka was that we built our gas chambers to accommodate 2,000 people at one time, whereas at Treblinka their ten gas chambers only accommodated 200 people each.

In Auschwitz even Picabia, viewing the logical consequences of his position, would have been forced to recognize the most delicious irony of them all: out of efficiency, to make nothingness, death.

We are all very easy with ourselves; today no one really believes in evil any more, even though we continually talk about thermonuclear war. Man's eternal optimism settles down on us, and we refuse to believe that Nazi horrors, Stalinist horrors, could come again.

But Stalinism was the aftermath of utopian revolution; and Nazism, with its industrial murders, its cool, abstracted technique of mass death, its aimless atrocities justified in the name of millenarian hope, was no reversion to medieval barbarism. Was it not the first of the truly modern, postindustrial political movements: passionate and active in personal style but masking an inner emptiness? Was it not the movement of alienated men driven to ultimate excesses by a frantic longing for sensation, any sensation, in a world where men had seemingly lost the ability to receive sensation, to make contact with their skins? Was it not an ideology wholly suited to a mechanical world—a mass movement, in fact, of the rootless, atomized, and lonely?

If the answer to these questions is yes, then we are all in trouble; because if what is coming is to Nazism as the new psychedelia, with its powerful drug technology, is to the old Dada, then there is going to be an awfully big bang someday. For the real trouble with romantic antirationalist movements is that at bottom they are nearly always sentimental in their view of mankind. Modern antirationalism has a long lineage, and in that

Resting on his Harley-Davidson, a member of an East Coast motorcycle club has a scowl on his face, a can of beer in his hand, and an Iron Cross over his heart.

lineage it is hard to find more than a few really evil men: long before futurism and Dada, we had Rousseau, Coleridge, and Byron, as well as Nietzsche and Baudelaire—all men who exalted feeling over thinking, action over reflection. The notion is always to get rid of distortions, to let free what lies in man, to replace fiction with truth, to give love. But what is it that lies in man? Love, surely, but rage and hate, too. And in modern man a desire to strike out, in despair . . . at what?

Modern life suffocates, but the hell of it may be that asphyxia is the price we pay for some modicum of order, some peace. Nothing, however, is so unconvincing as an argument by subtraction: if you did not have X, how sorry you would be.

If the hip movements are prophetic, and I for one believe they are, the wave of the future will not be rationalism and order, but the reverse. And that reverse will not forever remain apolitical, neutral to the world of action. What happens then?

If the years between the wars are any guide, we know the answer. Bertolt Brecht caught the mood of the interwar despair when he wrote in *Die Massnahme:*

What kind of medicine tastes bad to the
   dying?
What kind of depravity would you not
   bring about
In order to root out depravity forever?—
Yes, submerge us in filth,
But transform the world!

Poor Brecht! Desperately he pretended to be a good utopian rationalist, else he too would have been a Nazi. ❧

Edmund Stillman is a frequent contributor to Horizon. *His last article, "The Holy Terrors of Münster," appeared in the Summer, 1967, issue.*

THE MYSTERY GAME OF UR

The kings of ancient Sumer may be playing it still, but no one alive knows the rules

The remarkable work of art shown on the opposite page is the oldest game board in the world and now occupies a place of honor in the British Museum. It was last used about 2500 B.C. in the Sumerian city of Ur—the biblical Ur of the Chaldees.

Neither its name nor its rules have been preserved. For upward of four millenniums, while the very existence of Sumerian civilization was forgotten, the board lay undisturbed under a mound of ruins overlooking the lower reaches of the Euphrates. It was brought to light, finally, by the British archaeologist Sir Leonard Woolley, as part of the greatest hoard of art treasures ever discovered in Mesopotamia. As leader of the joint British Museum–University of Pennsylvania expedition to Ur in the 1920's, Sir Leonard excavated a series of mysterious mass graves—the tombs either of royal personages and their retainers or of priests and priestesses sacrificed to propitiate the gods at New Year's time.

In one of these tombs he found bodies of ten women carefully arranged in two rows: "they wore head-dresses of gold, lapis lazuli, and carnelian, and elaborate bead necklaces. . . . At the end of the row lay the remains of a wonderful harp, the wood of it decayed but its decoration intact . . . across the ruins of the harp lay the bones of the gold-crowned harpist."

A number of inlaid game-boards were among the treasures of Ur—this one, according to Sir Leonard, is "the most striking example found"—and they seem to have been a diversion of the upper classes, since the boards always turn up in rich or royal graves. Presumably they were placed in the tombs so that the dead would have a pastime with which to while away eternity in the next world.

A thing of beauty, needless to say, is a game forever, but the question remains, how

13	12	13
14	11	14
	10	
	9	
1	8	1
2	7	2
3	6	3
4	5	4

does one go about playing this one? That is still anybody's guess, at least until somebody finds the cuneiform equivalent of Hoyle. But why not, for once, a game in which no one knows the rules? An excellent analogy to life itself. The reader is therefore invited to invent his own set of rules: an exercise in limited omnipotence, the devising of a method for a microcosm.

Each of the Ur game-boards had its quota of buttonlike "men" and pyramid-shaped "dice." Apparently each player had seven men and six dice. The men are either of shell with lapis-lazuli dots or of black shale with shell dots. The dice, of which only a very few were found in various sites, are in the form of equilateral pyramids, each with two marked and two plain corners. There is no other evidence as to how the game was played, but the staff of the Department of Western Asiatic Antiquities at the British Museum suggests the outline of one method, based on the diagram at left.

Perhaps, so the reasoning goes, each player had to move his men along four private squares (1–4) up a common center track (squares 5–12), where a man could be knocked out if another landed on the same square, and then "home" off the board by way of the last two private squares (13–14). This theory leaves unexplained the elaborate pattern of each square. Could this superb inlay work have had nothing more than decorative significance? The Sumerians, we know, were a highly sophisticated folk when it came to the manipulation of numbers and symbols.

They invented cuneiform writing, and their method of keeping time is with us yet: 24 hours, 60 minutes, 60 seconds. Dividing a circle into 360 degrees is also a Sumerian idea.

In any case, the possibilities are unlimited: can you suggest a better formula?

The board, in its present state, is a monument to Sir Leonard's patience and archaeological skill. When he discovered it, the wooden base of the board had long since crumbled to dust. The technique he devised for preserving the mosaic is described in his report on the 1929–31 excavations at Ur:

"The board lay face upwards in the soil. With the decay of the wood the whole of the encrustation of the upper surface had sunk down into the void so left, while the strip-work along the sides remained sticking up above it; this collapse had resulted in the dislocation of much of the fine mosaic border, and the regularity of the surface was disturbed, the shell squares often lying at an angle and the lapis strips overlapping them; further, the end of the larger section had been broken and the three last plaques . . . and the right-hand plaque of the next row lay separated from each other. . . It was this broken end that we found first and probably some pieces of the strip edging were overlooked by us; when the presence of the object was recognized we worked along it a square or so at a time, pouring hot wax over it as we went, and finally the whole was secured with waxed cloth and lifted. It has not been taken to pieces and remade. The inside was cleaned and covered with waxed muslin and the cloth and wax removed from the face and then it was placed face downwards on a sheet of glass and by applying heat we were able to push the component parts down into their places. . ."

And he adds, in a typically meticulous footnote: "A few floated up in the liquid wax but could be at once pushed down into their holes." Perhaps archaeology, after all, is the most exciting of thinking men's games.

By FREDERIC V. GRUNFELD

IS MAN'S BRAIN AN EVOLUTIONARY MISTAKE?

A careless Nature has provided man with three brains: one reptilian, one lower mammalian, and his own higher mammalian brain—but they don't get along with one another. We must teach them how, our author argues, before their conflict leads man to genosuicide

I n one of the early chapters of Genesis there is an episode that has inspired countless religious painters. It is the scene where Abraham ties his son to a pile of wood and prepares to cut his throat with a knife, then burns him for the love of Jehovah. We all disapprove of cutting a child's throat for personal motives; the question is why so many have for so long approved of the insane gesture of Abraham. Or why we have accepted so much else that is savage and irrational. If we look without blinders at the history of the human race, we must recognize that a paranoid streak runs unbroken from the blood sacrifices of almost all prehistoric cultures to the mass exterminations of the twentieth century.

To put it vulgarly, we are led to suspect that there is somewhere a screw loose in the human mind, and always has been. To put it into more scientific language, we ought to give consideration to the possibility that somewhere along the line something has gone seriously wrong with the evolution of the nervous system of Homo sapiens.

The strategy of evolution, like any other strategy, is subject to trial and error. There is nothing particularly improbable in the assumption that man's native equipment, though superior to that of any known animal species, nevertheless may contain some serious fault in the circuitry of his most precious and delicate instrument—the

---

Nine years ago, with the publication of The Sleepwalkers, *Arthur Koestler began a trilogy designed to answer nothing less than the big question: How does the mind of man function?* HORIZON *has followed Mr. Koestler's inquiry through* The Act of Creation, *published in 1964, from which we took the essays "The Eureka Process" and "The Aesthetics of Snobbery," printed in our issues of Autumn, 1964, and Winter, 1965. In those essays Mr. Koestler was concerned with "the glory of man," the creativity of the human mind that is "responsible for the splendor of our cathedrals." In the concluding book of the cycle,* The Ghost in the Machine *(being published this spring by The Macmillan Co.), he deals with the pathology of the human mind that is responsible "for the gargoyles that decorate" the cathedrals. In his summation, which we print here, he maintains that the human brain is a victim of schizophysiology, an evolutionary defect that, if not cured promptly, threatens the very survival of the species.*

---

central nervous system.

Whether a skylark is happier than a rainbow trout is a nice debating point; both are stagnant species but well adapted to their ways of life, and to call them evolutionary mistakes because they have not got the brains to write poetry would be the height of *hubris.* When the biologist talks of evolutionary mistakes, he means something more tangible and precise: some obvious deviation from nature's own standards of engineering efficiency, a constructional fault that deprives an organ of its survival value—like the monstrous antlers of the Irish elk. Some turtles and insects are so topheavy that if in combat or by misadventure they fall on their backs, they cannot get up again, and starve to death—a grotesque error in construction that Kafka turned into a symbol of the human predicament. But before talking of man, I must discuss briefly two earlier evolutionary mistakes in brain building, both of which have had momentous consequences.

The first concerns the brain development of the arthropods, which, with more than seven hundred thousand known species, constitute by far the largest phylum of the animal kingdom. They range from microscopic mites,

By ARTHUR KOESTLER

Crocodile, horse, and man battle for supremacy. Does this fight go on every day in our own brains?

through centipedes, insects, and spiders, to ten-foot giant crabs; but they all have this in common, that *their brains are built around their gullets.* In vertebrates the brain and spinal cord are both dorsal—at the back of the alimentary canal. In invertebrates, however, the main nerve-chain runs *ventrally*—on the belly side of the animal. The chain terminates in a ganglionic mass *beneath* the mouth. This is the phylogenetically older part of the brain; whereas the newer and more sophisticated part of it developed *above* the mouth, in the vicinity of the eyes or other distance-receptors. Thus the alimentary tube passes through the midst of the evolving brain-mass; and this is very bad evolutionary strategy, because if the brain is to grow, the alimentary tube will be more and more compressed. To quote Walter Holbrook Gaskell's *The Origin of Vertebrates:*

Progress on these lines must result in a crisis, owing to the inevitable squeezing out of the food-channel by the increasing nerve-mass. . . . Truly, at the time when vertebrates first appeared, the direction and progress of variation in the Arthropoda was leading, owing to the manner in which the brain was pierced by the esophagus, to a terrible dilemma—either the capacity for taking in food without sufficient intelli-

gence to capture it, or intelligence sufficient to capture food and no power to consume it.

The dilemma seems to have been particularly acute for "the highest scorpion and spider-like animals, whose brain-mass has grown round and compressed the food-tube so that nothing but fluid pabulum can pass through into the stomach; the whole group have become blood-suckers." Another authority, Frederic Wood-Jones, comments:

To become a blood sucker is to become a failure. Phylogenetic senility comes with the specialization of blood sucking. Phylogenetic death is sure to follow. Here, then, is an end to the progress in brain building among the invertebrates. Faced with the awful problem of the alternatives of intellectual advance accompanied by the certainty of starvation, and intellectual stagnation accompanied by the inability of enjoying a good square meal, they must perforce elect the latter if they are to live. The invertebrates made a fatal mistake when they started to build their brains around the esophagus. Their attempt to develop big brains was a failure . . . Another start must be made.

The failure is reflected by the fact that even in the highest forms of invertebrates—the social insects—behavior is almost entirely governed by

instinct; learning by experience plays a relatively small part. And since all members of the beehive are descended from the same pair of parents, with no discernible varieties in heredity, they have little individuality: insects are not persons. Admiration for the marvelous organization of the beehive should not blind us to this fact. In vertebrates, on the other hand, as we ascend the evolutionary ladder, individual learning plays an increasing role compared to instinct—thanks to the increase in size and complexity of the brain, which was free to grow without imposing on us a diet of porridge.

The second cautionary tale concerns the marsupials, a class of pouched animals living in Australia. Almost every marsupial, from mouse to wolf, has a close counterpart in the placental series, but each is of an inferior "make" compared with its opposite number. Wood-Jones (himself an Australian) comments regretfully: ". . . They are failures. Wherever marsupial meets higher mammal, it is the marsupial that is circumvented by superior cunning and forced to retreat or to succumb. The fox, the cat, the dog, the rabbit, the rat and the mouse are all ousting their parallels in the marsupial phylum."

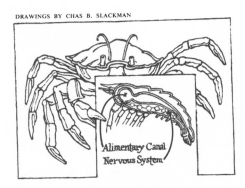

Alimentary Canal
Nervous System

"The strategy of evolution . . . is subject to trial and error," and it made a bad mistake with the arthropods by building their brains around their gullets. As a consequence, the crab, among others, faces the unlikely prospect of choking on its own intelligence.

The reason is simple: the brains of the marsupials are not only smaller, but of a vastly inferior construction. The ring-tailed opossum and the bush baby lemur are both arboreal and nocturnal animals and have certain similarities in size, appearance, and habits. But in the opossum, a marsupial, about one-third of the cerebral hemispheres is given to the sense of smell—sight, hearing, and all higher functions are crowded together in the remaining two-thirds. The placental lemur, on the other hand, has not only a larger brain, though its body is smaller than the opossum's, but the area devoted to smell in the lemur's brain has shrunk to relative insignificance, giving way, as it should, to areas serving functions more vital to an arboreal creature.

When the marsupials took to the trees, smell ought to have become unimportant to them compared with the distance receptors—sight and hearing —and their nervous systems ought to have reflected the change. But in contrast to our ancestors the placental tree dwellers, this change failed to take place in the marsupials. Moreover, an important component is lacking in the brain of the higher marsupials, the so-called *corpus callosum*. This is a conspicuous nerve tract that, in placentals, connects the "new" (nonolfactory) areas of the right and left cerebral hemispheres. It obviously plays a vital integrative part, though the details of its functioning are still problematical,

and its absence from the marsupial brain seems to have been a principal factor in their arrested development.

The point at which that development comes to an end is the koala bear. It is, to quote Wood-Jones again, "the largest and most perfectly adapted tree-dwelling marsupial. In bulk we may compare it with the Patas monkey." But, compared to the monkey, the koala cuts a very poor figure: "In the koala the tree-climber has become a tree-clinger. Hands have turned into hooks; and fingers are not used for plucking fruit or leaves or testing novel objects, but for fixing the animal, by virtue of the long curved claws, to the tree upon which it clings."

It cannot do otherwise, because its principal sense is still smell, which is of little use in an arboreal creature. Like Quoodle, the koala thinks with his nose. His brain weighs only one-seventh of the monkey's, and most of it is occupied by the smell area that in the monkey has virtually vanished; in addition, the nonsmell areas of the koala have no *corpus callosum* to connect them. The koala is the end of the marsupial line of evolution, left behind clinging to his eucalyptus tree like a discarded hypothesis—while his monkey cousin is only the beginning of the evolution from primate to man.

But before congratulating ourselves on having such a superior brain—one that does not strangle our esophagus

or condemn us to live by smell—we ought to pause and examine the possibility that man, too, might carry a constructional fault inside his skull, perhaps even more serious than the arthropod and marsupial precedents: a constructional error that potentially threatens his extinction, but that might still be corrected by a supreme effort of self-repair.

The first reason for this suspicion is the extraordinary rapidity of the evolutionary growth of the human brain—a feat, as we know, unique in evolutionary history. Let me quote from Charles Judson Herrick's *The Evolution of Human Nature:*

The history of civilization is a record of slow but dramatic enrichment of human life interspersed with episodes of wanton destruction of all the accumulated riches of property and spiritual values. These episodic reversions to bestiality seem to be increasing in virulence and in the magnitude of the resulting disasters until now we are threatened with the loss of everything that has been won in our struggle for the better life.

In view of this record it has been suggested that the enlargement of the human brain has gone so fast and so far that the result is actually pathological. Normal behavior depends upon the preservation of a balanced interplay between integrating and disintegrating factors and between the total pattern and local partial patterns. So, it is claimed, the human cortex is a sort of tumorous overgrowth that has got so big that its functions are out of normal control

The opossum, at left, is larger than the lemur but has a brain better suited to smelling than thinking. Like all marsupials, it is stupider than its placental counterpart. The koala bear, which "thinks with his nose... is the end of the marsupial line of evolution, left behind clinging to his eucalyptus tree like a discarded hypothesis ..."

and "race" erratically like a steam engine that has lost its governor.

This ingenious theory was published by Morley Roberts and quoted with apparent approval by [William Morton] Wheeler. Their arguments seem to be plausible in view of the past history of wars, revolutions, and crumbled empires, and the present world-wide turmoil that threatens total destruction of civilization. But the theory is neurological nonsense.

In the form stated here it certainly is. It cannot be the *size* of the cortex alone that "puts its function out of normal control." We must look for a more plausible cause.

The cause that contemporary research seems to indicate is not increase in size, but *insufficient co-ordination* between the phylogenetically old areas of our brain and the new, specifically human areas that were superimposed on it with such unseemly haste. Thus lack of co-ordination causes, to use a phrase coined by Paul MacLean, a kind of "dichotomy in the function of the phylogenetically old and new cortex that might account for differences between emotional and intellectual behavior." While "our intellectual functions are carried on in the newest and most highly developed part of the brain, our affective behavior continues to be dominated by a relatively crude and primitive system. This situation provides a clue to understanding the difference between what we 'feel' and what we 'know.'"

The distinction between "knowing" and "feeling," between reason and emotion, goes back to the Greeks. Aristotle in *De Anima* pointed to visceral sensations as the *substance* of emotion and contrasted them with the *form*, i.e., the ideational content of the emotion. The intimate connection between emotion and the viscera is a matter of common experience and has always been taken for granted by laymen and physicians alike: we know that emotional arousal affects heartbeat and pulse; that fear stimulates the sweat glands, grief the tear glands; and that the respiratory, digestive, not to mention the reproductive, systems are all involved in the experience of emotion. So much so that the word "visceral" was originally used to refer to strong emotional feelings, including fear ("he has no guts") and pity ("the bowels of mercy").

As one would expect, the viscera are controlled by a phylogenetically very ancient structure in the brain stem, the region of the hypothalamus (*thalamos:* Greek for inner chamber, or woman's apartment). This is the crucial area—in close proximity to the pituitary gland and to the vestiges of the primitive smell-brain—which regulates visceral and glandular functions beyond voluntary control and is intimately connected with emotional experience.

Let us consider the question of how these archaic structures, and the archaic feelings to which they give rise, get along with the brand-new structures and functions in our brains. The following excerpts lead straight into the problem; they are from two medical papers by Professor MacLean.

Man finds himself in the predicament that Nature has endowed him essentially with three brains which, despite great differences in structure, must function together and communicate with one another. The oldest of these brains is basically reptilian. The second has been inherited from lower mammals, and the third is a late mammalian development, which in its culmination in primates, has made man peculiarly man.

Speaking allegorically of these three brains within a brain, we might imagine that when the psychiatrist bids the patient to lie on the couch, he is asking him to stretch out alongside a horse and a crocodile. The crocodile may be willing and ready to shed a tear and the horse to neigh and whinny, but when they are encouraged to express their troubles in words, it soon becomes evident that their inability is beyond the help of language training. Little wonder that the patient who has personal responsibility for these animals and who must serve as their mouthpiece is sometimes accused of being full of resistances and reluctant to talk ... The reptilian brain is filled with ancestral lore and ancestral memories and is faithful in doing what its ancestors say, but it is not a very good brain for facing up to new situations. It is as though it were neurosis-bound to an ancestral superego.

In evolution one first sees the beginning of emancipation from the ancestral superego with the appearance of the lower

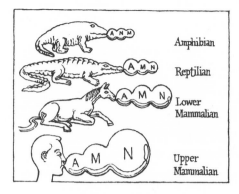

mammalian brain, which Nature builds on top of the reptilian brain. . . . investigations of the last twenty years have shown that the lower mammalian brain plays a fundamental role in emotional behavior. . . . it has a greater capacity than the reptilian brain for learning new approaches and solutions to problems on the basis of immediate experience. But like the reptilian brain, it does not have the ability . . . to put its feelings into words.

In the remainder of this discussion I shall lean heavily on MacLean's experimental work and theoretical conclusions (though deviating from the latter in minor details). "In its evolution," he writes, "the brain of man retains the hierarchical organization of the three basic types which can be conveniently labeled as reptilian, paleomammalian and neo-mammalian. . . . And there is ample evidence that all three types have their own special subjective, cognitive (problem-solving) memory and other parallel functions."

The cortex has three basic subdivisions. MacLean calls them archicortex, mesocortex, and neocortex, co-ordinated respectively with the reptilian, primitive mammalian, and neomammalian brain. But the spatial arrangement of these three main cortical divisions inside our skulls is not easy to explain or visualize. MacLean proposed a simplified model in the form of an inflatable toy balloon with three distinct segments (see diagram above).

A, M, and N stand for archi, meso,

and neo cortex. "The uninflated balloon represents the situation found in the amphibian. With the appearance of the reptile, there is a ballooning out of the archicortex . . . a considerable expansion of the mesocortex. During the phylogeny of the mammal one of the most striking events of all evolution occurs. This is the great ballooning out of the neocortex. In the process, the archicortex and the greater part of the mesocortex are folded like two concentric rings into the limbic lobe and are relegated, as it were, to the cellar of the brain."

The two in-folded rings together form a large convolution, the so-called limbic lobe of the cerebral cortex. "Limbic" means "hemming in," "forming a border around"; the term was used in 1878 by the great brain-mapper Paul Broca, because the limbic convolution surrounds the brain stem —the central core. In fact the limbic cortex is so closely connected to the brain stem that together they constitute a functionally integrated system—the limbic system, with its reptilian and lower mammalian features. The limbic system may thus be loosely called the "old brain," in contrast to the neocortical system, or "new brain."

This is surely an odd state of affairs. If the evidence had not taught us the contrary, we would expect an evolutionary development that gradually transformed the primitive old brain into a more sophisticated instrument—

as it transformed claw into hand, gill into lung. Instead, evolution superimposed a new, superior structure on an old one, with partly overlapping functions and without providing the new with a clear-cut, hierarchic control over the old—thus inviting confusion and conflict. Let us have a closer look at this dichotomy between the limbic and neocortical systems.

The ancient, limbic system has three principal characteristics: (a) its microscopic structure is coarse and primitive compared with that of the neocortex; (b) its basic pattern is still essentially the same as in the lower mammals; (c) in contrast to the new cortex, the limbic system is intimately connected by two-way neural pathways—fibers as thick as a pencil—with the hypothalamus and other centers in the brain stem concerned with visceral sensations and emotional reactions, including sex, hunger, fear, and aggression (so much so that the limbic system once bore the name "the visceral brain"). The term was changed because it gave the impression that it was *only* concerned with the viscera; whereas in fact the ancient, limbic cortex, as we shall see, also has its own mental processes: it emotes and *thinks*—though not in verbal concepts.

The limbic system may be compared to a primitive television screen that combines, and often confuses, projections from the internal, visceral en-

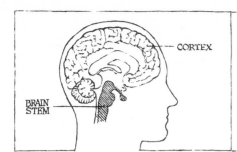

		BRAIN STEM _medulla oblongata_		
LIMBIC SYSTEM "OLD BRAIN"		_pons_ _mid brain_ _thalami_		
		THE CORTEX OF THE BRAIN		
		REPTILIAN	_ARCHICORTEX_	LIMBIC LOBE or
		PALEO- or LOWER MAMMALIAN	_MESOCORTEX_	LIMBIC CORTEX
		NEO- or HIGHER MAMMALIAN	_NEOCORTEX_	"NEW BRAIN"

In man "evolution superimposed a new, superior structure [the neocortex] on an old one [the limbic system], with partly overlapping functions and without providing the new with a clear-cut, hierarchic control over the old—thus inviting confusion and conflict."

vironment with the external environment. As MacLean says:

Such a cortex must have offered some of the confusion of a double exposure. In any event, it could not have been altogether satisfactory, because when Nature proceeded to develop the neomammalian brain, she constructed a progressively bigger and finer type of screen, which gave predominantly a picture of the outside world made up of impressions from the eye, the ear, and the surface of the body. . . . But Nature in her frugality did not discard the old screen. Since it seemed adequate for smelling, tasting, and feeling what is going on inside the body, she has kept the filaments in the tube of the old screen glowing night and day.

However, the old brain is not merely concerned with taste, smell, and visceral sensations, leaving the new to turn its gaze outward: that would be an idyllic distribution of labor. The Papez theory of emotions originated in the study of pathological conditions in which the "old tube" interferes with the new and tends to usurp its functions. Papez noted that damage to the limbic system caused a variety of symptoms, which primarily affected the emotional behavior of animal and man. An extreme case is the terrible disease of rabies, whose virus appears to have a predilection for the limbic system, and in which "the patient is subject to paroxysms of rage and terror."

The human clinical material is lim-

ited, and electroencephalography is a recent invention; thus most of the evidence is provided by experimentation on animals. In experiments with monkeys electrodes have been implanted in the brain, permitting low-voltage stimulation of precisely defined points. Stimulation of certain loci in the limbic system caused penile erection or ejaculation in males; stimulation of other points caused feeding reactions—chewing and salivation; yet other areas elicited exploratory, aggressive-defensive, or fearful behavior. (It should be pointed out that these are painless experiments and that monkeys with electrodes implanted in the so-called pleasure centers quickly and willingly learn to stimulate themselves by pressing a lever that activates the current.) However, excitement of one kind readily spills over to adjacent points that arouse emotions of another kind. Thus oral activity—chewing, sniffing, salivating—may combine with aggression; aggressive display with sex; sex with oral activity. Feeding often produces erection in babies and dogs; and some other aspects of doggy behavior also fall far below Victorian standards.

Here again, the contrast between old and new cortex provides an unexpected clue, and an added dimension to the psychoanalytical approach. On the new television screen (the sensory cortex) the body is represented in the well-known form of a little homunculus, like the one shown in all textbooks, on

which the mouth and the anal-genital regions are placed correctly at opposite ends of the projection area. In the old, lower mammalian brain, however, "Nature apparently found it necessary to bend the limbic lobe upon itself in order to afford the olfactory sense close participation in both oral and anogenital functions."

This is a truly unexpected vindication of Freud's theory of infantile sexuality. It is at the same time a reminder that the survival of the lower mammalian brain in our heads is not metaphor but fact. In the sexual, as in all other contexts, maturation seems to mean a transition from the domination of the old brain toward the domination of the new. But quite apart from emotional upsets and pathological conditions, the transition even in the normal person can never be complete. _The schizophysiology is built into our species._

As long as we believed that our species as such was virtually immortal, with an astronomical life span before it, we could afford to wait patiently for that change of heart that, gradually or suddenly, would make love, peace, and sweet reason prevail. But we no longer have that assurance of immortality, nor the unlimited time to wait for the moment when the lion will lie down with the lamb, the Arab with the Israeli, and the commissar with the Yogi.

The conclusions, if we dare to draw them, are quite simple. Our biological

"The limbic system may be compared to a primitive television screen that combines, and often confuses, projections from the internal, visceral environment with the external environment."

evolution to all intents and purposes came to a standstill in Cro-Magnon days. Since we cannot in the foreseeable future expect the necessary change in human nature to arise by way of a spontaneous mutation, that is, by natural means, we must induce it by artificial means. We can only hope to survive as a species by developing techniques that supplant biological evolution. We must search for a cure for the schizophysiology inherent in man's nature, and for the resulting split in our minds, which led to the situation in which we find ourselves.

I believe that if we fail to find this cure, the old paranoid streak in man, combined with his new powers of destruction, must sooner or later lead to genosuicide. But I also believe that the cure is almost within reach of contemporary biology and that with the proper concentration of efforts it might be produced within the lifetime of the generation now entering on the scene.

I am aware that this sounds overoptimistic in contrast with the seemingly overpessimistic views just expressed on the prospect ahead of us if we persist in carrying on in our paranoiac ways. I do not think these apprehensions are exaggerated, and I do not think that the idea of a cure for Homo sapiens is utopian. It is not inspired by science fiction, but is based on a realistic assessment of the recent advances in several convergent branches of the life sciences. They do not provide a cure,

but they indicate the area of research that may produce it.

I am also aware that any proposal that involves "artificial tampering with human nature" is bound to provoke strong emotional resistances. These are partly based on prejudice and partly on a healthy aversion toward further intrusions into the privacy and sanctity of the individual by the excesses of social engineering, character engineering, various forms of brainwashing, and other threatening aspects of the air-conditioned nightmare surrounding us. On the other hand, ever since the first hunter wrapped his shivering frame in the hide of a dead animal, man has been tampering with his own nature—creating for himself an artificial environment that has gradually transformed the face of the planet, and an artificial mode of existence without which he can no longer survive. There is no turning back on housing, clothing, artificial heating, cooked food; nor on spectacles, hearing aids, forceps, artificial limbs, anesthetics, antiseptics, prophylactics, vaccines, and so forth.

We start tampering with human nature almost from the moment a baby is born, for one of the first routine measures is the universal practice of dropping a solution of silver nitrate into the baby's eyes to protect it against *ophthalmia neonatorum*, a form of conjunctivitis frequently leading to blindness, caused by gonococci that, unknown to

her, may have lurked in the mother's genital tract. This is followed later on by preventive vaccinations, compulsory in most civilized countries, against smallpox, typhoid, and so on.

A less well known case of tampering is the prevention of goiter and of a certain variety of cretinism associated with it. When I was a child and was taken for the holidays to the Alps, the number of inhabitants of mountain valleys who had monstrous swellings in front of their necks, and the number of cretinous children in their families was quite frightening. Today there is not a single case of goiter in the Tyrolean village where I spend part of the year, nor in the neighboring valleys. It has been found that goiter is associated with a deficiency of iodine in the thyroid gland and that the water in regions where the disease used to be endemic was hard and poor in iodine. Thus iodine was periodically added in small quantities to the drinking water or diet of the children, and goiter became virtually a thing of the past.

Evidently man, or a certain breed of man, has not been biologically equipped to live in environments with iodine-poor water, or to cope with the virus of smallpox and the deadly micro-organisms of malaria or sleeping sickness. If we reverse the situation, we find that some microbes are equally ill equipped for resisting other species of microorganisms, which we call antibiotics. Now microbes seem to have an enor-

"these are painless experiments
and monkeys . . . quickly
and willingly learn
to stimulate themselves by
pressing a lever
that activates the current."

mous mutation rate (or some other method of hereditary adaptation), for within a few years they have evolved new drug-resistant strains. We humans cannot perform such evolutionary feats. But we can *simulate* major adaptive mutations by putting drops into the eyes of the newborn to protect them from enemies against which our natural defenses are inadequate.

Can we invent a similar remedy for the schizophysiology of our nervous system, for the paranoid streak in man that has made such an appalling mess of our history?

The neurophysiological evidence indicates, as we have seen, a dissonance between the reactions of neocortex and limbic system. Instead of functioning as integral parts in a hierarchic order, they lead a kind of agonized coexistence. To revert to an earlier metaphor; the rider has never gained complete control of the horse, and the horse asserts its whims in the most objectionable ways. We have also seen that the horse—the limbic system—has direct access to the emotion-generating, viscerally oriented centers in the hypothalamus; but the rider has no direct access to them. Moreover, the stirrups and reins by which the rider is meant to control the horse are inadequate. To quote MacLean once more: "On the basis of neuronographic studies there appear to be no extensive 'associational' connections between the limbic and the neo cortex." There is no ana-

tomical evidence for the intricate "loops within loops" of feedbacks, of the delicate interplay of excitation and inhibition that characterizes the nervous system in general. "Both horse and man are very much alive to one another and to their environment, yet communication between them is limited. Both derive information and act upon it in a different way."

To go on preaching sweet reason to an inherently unreasonable species is, as history shows, a fairly hopeless task. Evolution has let us down; we can only hope to survive if we develop techniques that supplant it by inducing the necessary changes in human nature.

John Saunders, former Chancellor of the San Francisco Medical Center of the University of California, said at a 1961 symposium on "Control of the Mind":

The great technological skill and ingenuity of the modern chemist has provided the medical scientist and the physician with an abundant array of new chemical compounds of varying and diverse structure which influence the central nervous system to distort, accelerate, or depress the mental state and behavioral characteristics of the individual. The conference emphasized that many of these chemical agents possess a highly selective action on particular and discrete parts of the nervous system—so much so as to permit from an examination of their actions in man and animals an arrangement in order and rank. Those chemical agents thus offer, by a considera-

tion of the relationships between chemical structure and biological action, the possibility of providing a vast array of drugs influencing the specific activity of the brain. Indeed, since such agents may either potentiate or attenuate one another, exhibit overlap in their actions, and demonstrate polarity in their effects on the brain, the very strong possibility is suggested of a full spectrum of chemical agents which can be used for the control of the mind in the majority of its activities.

. . . Here at our disposal, to be used wisely or unwisely, is an increasing array of agents that manipulate human beings. . . . It is now possible to act directly on the individual to modify his behavior instead of, as in the past, indirectly through modification of the environment. This, then, constitutes a part of what Aldous Huxley has called "The Final Revolution" . . .

I must comment on the last paragraph in this quotation. Huxley was haunted by the fear that this "Final Revolution," brought about by the combined effect of drugs and the mass media, could create "within a generation or so for entire societies a sort of painless concentration camp of the mind, in which people will have lost their liberties in the enjoyment of a dictatorship without tears." In other words, the state of affairs described in *Brave New World*. As an antidote Huxley advocated the use of mescaline and other psychedelic drugs to guide us along the eightfold path toward cosmic consciousness, mystic enlightenment, and artistic creativity.

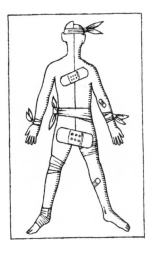

"Can we invent a . . . remedy for the schizophysiology of our nervous system, for the paranoid streak in man that has made such an appalling mess of our history?"

I have long been an admirer of Huxley's personality and work, but in his last years I profoundly disagreed with him; and the points of disagreement will help to clarify the issue.

In *Heaven and Hell*, praising the benefits of mescaline, Huxley offered this advice to modern man in search of his soul: "Knowing . . . what are the chemical conditions of transcendental experience, the aspiring mystic should turn for technical help to the specialists —in pharmacology, in biochemistry, in physiology and neurology. . ."

Now this is precisely what I do *not* mean by the positive uses of psychopharmacology. In the first place, experimenting with mescaline or with LSD 25 does involve serious risks. But quite apart from this, it is fundamentally wrong, and naïve, to expect that drugs can present the mind with gratis gifts—put into it something that is not already there. Neither mystic insights nor philosophic wisdom nor creative power can be provided by pill or injection. The psychopharmacist cannot *add* to the faculties of the brain—but he can *eliminate* obstructions and blockages that impede their proper use. He cannot aggrandize us—but he can, within limits, normalize us; he cannot put additional circuits into the brain, but he can, again within limits, improve the co-ordination between existing ones, attenuate conflicts, prevent the blowing of fuses, and ensure a steady power supply. That is all the

help we can ask for—but if we were able to obtain it, the benefits to mankind would be incalculable; it would be the "Final Revolution" in a sense opposite to Huxley's—the breakthrough from maniac to man.

The "we" in the previous sentence is not meant to refer to patients in the psychiatric ward or on the therapist's couch. Psychopharmacology will no doubt play an increasing part in the treatment of mental disorders in the clinical sense, but that is not the point. What we are concerned with is a cure for the paranoic streak in what we call normal people, i.e., mankind as a whole: an artificially simulated, adaptive mutation to bridge the rift between the phylogenetically old and new brain, between instinct and intellect, emotion and reason. If it is within our reach to increase man's suggestibility, it will soon be within our reach to do the opposite—to counteract misplaced devotion and that militant enthusiasm, both murderous and suicidal, that we see reflected in the pages of the daily newspaper. The most urgent task of biochemistry is the search for a remedy in the "increasing range," as Saunders put it, "of the spectrum of chemical agents which can be used for the control of the mind." It is not utopian to believe that it can and will be done. Our present tranquilizers, barbiturates, stimulants, antidepressants, and combinations thereof are merely a first step toward a more sophisticated range of

aids to promote a co-ordinated, harmonious state of mind. Not the unruffled ataraxia sought by the Stoics, not the ecstasy of the dancing dervish, nor the pop-nirvana created by Huxley's "soma" pills—but a state of dynamic equilibrium in which thought and emotion are reunited and hierarchic order is restored.

I am aware that "control of the mind" and "manipulating human beings" have sinister undertones. Who is to control the controls, manipulate the manipulators? Assuming that we succeed in synthetizing a hormone that acts as a mental stabilizer on the lines indicated—how are we to propagate its global use to induce that beneficial mutation? Are we to ram it down people's throats, or put it into the tap water?

The answer seems obvious. No legislation, no compulsory measures, were needed to persuade Greeks and Romans to partake of "the juice of the grape that gives joy and oblivion." Sleeping pills, pep pills, tranquilizers, have, for better or worse, spread across the world with a minimum of publicity or official encouragement. They have spread because people liked their effect and even accepted their unpleasant or harmful aftereffects. A mental stabilizer would produce neither euphoria, nor sleep, nor mescaline visions, nor cabbagelike equanimity—it would in fact have no noticeably specific effect, except to promote cerebral co-ordina-

The three brains, represented by man, horse, and crocodile, find repose in a Peaceable Kingdom

tion and harmonize thought and emotion; in other words, to restore the integrity of the split hierarchy. Its use would spread because people like feeling healthy rather than unhealthy in body or mind. It would spread as vaccination has spread, and contraception has spread, not by coercion but by enlightened self-interest.

The first noticeable result would perhaps be a sudden drop in the crime and suicide rates in certain regions and social groups where the new Pill had become fashionable. From here on the developments are as unpredictable as the consequences of James Watt's or Pasteur's discoveries were. Some Swiss canton might decide, after a public referendum, to add the new substance to the chlorine in the water supply for a trial period, and other countries might follow their example. Or there might be an international fashion among the young, replacing weirdy-beards. In one way or the other the mutation would get under way.

It is possible that totalitarian countries would try to resist it. But today even iron curtains have become porous: hot jazz, miniskirts, discotheques, and other bourgeois inventions are spreading irresistibly. When the ruling elite started experimenting with the new medicine and discovered that it made them see things in an altogether different light, then, and only then, would the world be ripe for a global disarmament conference that is not a sinister farce. And should there be a transitional period during which one side alone went ahead with the cure while the other persisted in its paranoid ways, there would be none of the risks of unilateral disarmament involved; on the contrary, the mutated side would be stronger because more rational in its long-term policies, less frightened, and less hysterical.

I do not think this is science fiction; and I am confident that the type of reader to whom I speak will not think so either. Every writer has a favorite type of imaginary reader, a friendly but highly critical phantom whose opinion is the only one that matters and with whom he is engaged in a continuous, exhausting dialogue. I feel sure, as I said, that my friendly phantom reader has sufficient imagination to extrapolate from the recent, breath-taking advances of biology into the future and to concede that the solution outlined here is in the realm of the possible. What worries me is that he will not like it, that he might be repelled and disgusted by the idea that we should rely for our salvation on molecular chemistry instead of a spiritual rebirth. I share his distress, but I see no alternative. I hear him exclaim: "By trying to sell us your pills, you are adopting that crudely materialistic attitude and naïve scientific *hubris* that you pretend to oppose." I still oppose it. But I do not believe that it is materialistic to take a realistic view of the condition of man, nor is it *hubris* to feed thyroid extracts to children who would otherwise grow into cretins. To use our brain to cure its own shortcomings seems to me a brave and dedicated enterprise. Like the reader, I would prefer to set my hopes on moral persuasion by word and example. But we are a mentally sick race, and as such, deaf to persuasion. It has been tried from the age of the prophets to the age of Albert Schweitzer; and the result has been, as Swift said, that "we have just enough religion to make us hate, but not enough to make us love one another." That applies to all religions, theistic or secular, whether taught by Moses or Marx or Mao Tse-tung; and Swift's anguished cry, "not die here in a rage, like a poisoned rat in a hole" has acquired an urgency as never before.

Nature has let us down. God seems to have left the receiver off the hook, and time is running out. To hope for salvation to be synthesized in the laboratory may seem materialistic, crankish, or naïve; but to tell the truth, there is a Jungian twist to it—for it reflects the ancient alchemist's dream to concoct the *elixir vitae*. What we expect from it, however, is not eternal life, or the transformation of base metal into gold, but the transformation of Homo maniacus into Homo sapiens. When man decides to take his fate into his own hands, that possibility will be within reach.

THE FATE OF JACOB STALIN

Jacob Stalin as a prisoner of war, seen in a Nazi Propaganda Office photograph.

The Russian dictator's eldest son was captured by the Germans in 1941. Here, a Polish officer who befriended him in a prisoner-of-war camp tells the story of his imprisonment and execution

By MICHAEL A. BUDEK

I first saw him on the parade square of Oflag Xc at a prisoner-of-war roll call on a cold and cloudy morning late in 1942, a youngish man of middle height with dark, tousled hair and a long and sullen face. He wore a Russian military greatcoat that looked as if he had slept many nights in it, navy-blue breeches, and jack boots far too big for him. We, the Polish officers, were lined up on the right of the square, followed by Belgians, French, Yugoslavs, and finally the French Jews, who were kept apart. Just as our battalion commander, Captain Schulze—a Mecklenburg landowner and reserve officer—began to call the roll, four guards appeared with the dark-haired stranger.

"Your place is there with the staff officers' company, Colonel Antonov," Schulze told him, pointing to the front rank of Polish officers.

"I am no Colonel Antonov," the stranger shouted excitedly in Russian. "I am Lieutenant Yakov Dzhugashvili!"

To the other prisoners that name meant nothing, but we Poles knew at once that this rather sickly young man was Stalin's eldest son. After the roll call was over, we talked with him. He told us he had been captured in July of 1941 near Liozno, while the Germans were driving through Smolensk toward Moscow. At that time he had been in command of a field artillery battery. He had been wounded and his battery overrun by the Germans, who would have killed him if a Russian soldier had not warned them that the wounded officer was Stalin's son. After the interrogation he was sent to a prisoner-of-war hospital and then, though still in poor health, to our Oflag Xc in Lübeck.

Oflag Xc, commanded by an old, monocled hussar officer, Colonel Freiherr von Wachtmeister, was one of the two special camps that the Germans had built for high-ranking officers and lower-rank officers who came from noted families or who were considered dangerous. Surrounded by a double line of barbed-wire fence thirty feet high, and by a series of turrets with machine guns, it contained about twenty-six hundred prisoners. From the turrets guards watched the whole camp day and night through binoculars and were instructed to shoot anyone who approached the "warning wire."

Within our group were about twenty Belgian generals, including the commander in chief, General Vandenbergh, as well as serving members of parliament and several international financiers. Among the two hundred and fifty or so Poles was the chief of the Polish general staff, General Piskor. Of the several hundred French officers, many bore internationally known names, the most conspicuous among them being René Rothschild and Lieutenant Vigée Lebrun, the son of the French president.

It was natural enough that the son of the Russian dictator should end up at Oflag Xc. But that I, a reserve horse artillery captain, should have been there among all the generals and colonels and counts came about through my chance and brief meeting with Herbert Hoover in 1919, when he was head of the children's relief mission in Europe.

As a young officer in the new Polish Army, speaking five languages, I had been appointed a liaison officer with the Allied Military Mission and afterward assigned to duty with children's relief. When Hoover came to Gorlice shortly before his return to the United States, I happened to be at the railroad station in uniform. Being the only person present with a camera, I took several snapshots of him at the railroad station. He walked over to me, shook hands, and asked me to send him copies of the pictures.

Not until 1926, when I had left the army to become a lawyer, did I remember my promise and send the snapshots. I then visited some of the families who had received the American supplies seven years before, to see what the children now looked like. In one village I found a peasant's hut with the usual small altar in the corner but with a battered empty tin of American condensed milk among the plaster saints. When I asked the peasant why the tin was there, he said it was out of respect for the American mission that had saved the children from starvation. I took a photograph of the altar and sent it to Hoover.

In 1937 Hoover paid a visit to Poland, and to my surprise I received an invitation from the president of the republic to attend an official dinner in Warsaw for the former American president. Hoover gave me a small memento —a theatre ticket on the back of which he had written: "With best wishes, Herbert C. Hoover."

In August, 1939, I was called back to the army to command a territorial cavalry squadron in defense of Gdynia. On September 14 I was wounded, and while in the hospital was taken prisoner. Eventually I was sent to Oflag Xa in Itzehoe, a camp in northwestern Germany containing about six thousand war prisoners.

In Itzehoe I learned that my wife and children were in distress in Cracow. There was not much I could do, but I did know two addresses abroad —one in England and Hoover's in California. Wanting to help my family in any way I could, I sent an official prisoner-of-war card to England and to California, saying that I had been wounded and that my wife was still at the old address. The cards did not help my family, but a few months later I received a huge parcel of food marked from Mr. Herbert Hoover. The name caused a stir among the Germans, and I was called to the camp commander and asked what my connection was with a former American president. I refused to say, but the Germans must have thought me an important person, for shortly afterward I was sent, along with two or three hundred others, to the special international camp at Lübeck.

After his explosive arrival in our camp, Stalin's son remained a curiosity. We never referred to him as "Dzhugashvili" but as "Stalin's son," and then simply "Stalin." Since Polish-Russian relations had been resumed, he declared it his duty to stay with the Poles and reported to General Piskor, introducing himself and asking advice as to how he should behave.

General Piskor asked Lieutenant Colonel Mazdzenski to take care of Stalin and offered the Russian two of the American Red Cross parcels that every officer in the camp got twice a month. Stalin refused to accept them, saying that he did not want to eat American food under any circumstances.

From the time of his arrival, Stalin was constantly invited to our prisoner parties, which he attended regularly even though he found himself exposed to innumerable questions about high-level world policy, about which he seemed to know little or nothing. We were aware that his relations with his father were not the best and had not been for some time, although we did not then know the cause of their estrangement. In spite of the fact that he knew less than most of us about world politics, he did his best to answer each question and was never impatient at being forced to repeat himself.

Stalin was billeted in the corner room of Barracks 11, next to Captain Robert Blum, the son of the former French premier. The barracks, a wooden building apart from the others and close to the barbed-wire fence, had huge windows through which the German guards could observe both of the prisoners.

At the beginning of his stay in camp, Stalin could move anywhere he liked, though always guarded by a specially assigned watchman. Then, because of a ridiculous incident, he lost his privilege of free movement. The incident occurred when he went to a tea party in Polish Barracks Number 3, guarded by a German who was old and short-sighted and wore thick glasses. During the course of the tea party, one of the Polish officers got up, said good-bye to the others, left the barracks, and started his daily stroll around the camp.

After a while he noticed that he was being followed by the nearsighted guard. Realizing that the man could be severely punished for abandoning Stalin, the Polish officer turned to the guard and told him, "You are mistaken, I am not Stalin!"

The stubborn guard insisted that the Pole was Stalin, until a burst of laughter from the other Polish officers convinced him of his mistake. "My God," he said, his face gone white, "I shall be shot!" "Go to barracks three, room ten, and there you will find your Stalin," the Polish officer told him. The guard followed this advice and found his Stalin, still there drinking tea.

The whole incident would perhaps have remained unnoticed by the Germans, but because it was talked of so much in the camp, the commandant learned about it. From that time on, Stalin was restricted in his movements, although he could still receive other officers in his room.

My duty in the camp was to supervise the preparation and distribution of all rations. A second and more private duty was to barter with the German guards. In exchange for American or English cigarettes that the other officers entrusted to me, I acquired letter forms and other documents necessary for anyone trying to escape. During my whole stay in the camp kitchen, I dealt in this kind of smuggling without once being caught. Instant coffee was the most precious camp money; in exchange for it we managed to get parts for three radio receiving-sets, which we were able to keep concealed in spite of searches by the Germans and through which we kept in touch with the world outside. Whatever the language, one of us was able to understand it; altogether we spoke sixty-four languages, including a number of Asiatic and African dialects. One Belgian major spoke twenty-three languages.

Since I spoke only five, I was rather surprised when Stalin, who appeared every day in the kitchen to collect his food ration, asked if I would tutor him.

The kitchen was hardly a place for conversation, and I agreed to visit him in his room. Shortly afterward I was ordered to report to General Piskor, who told me: "Because of your previous confidential work as a liaison officer, I have decided at the request of Lieutenant Dzhugashvili to assign you to him as a teacher of foreign languages."

I thought Stalin would like to learn English because it was the most widely spoken language in the camp; but when I suggested this his face darkened, and he replied that he was not interested in English at all. What he wanted to learn was German. I thought perhaps he was planning to escape and wanted to pick up a few useful German words and phrases to help him on his way. But to my astonishment he gave me another reason. After the war, he said, many German war prisoners would be employed in Russia, and since he was an engineer by profession it would be extremely useful for him to know German. I accepted his answer and asked nothing about any escape plans. And we began our German lessons.

Stalin, though he studied hard, had considerable difficulty in both pronunciation and grammar. He showed continued astonishment over the intricacies of construction and wondered why Germans—"such a clever folk"—had such a ponderous vocabulary. During one of our lessons a prisoner in the same barracks was playing the "Song of the Volga Boatmen." I told Stalin that this song had become popular everywhere in the world and that I had often heard it played in South America. He didn't like it much, saying that under the communist regime the music was gay and spontaneous, whereas under the czars they sang only sad and hopeless songs.

Sometimes he would talk to me about his lost motherland, saying that no land in the world was more beautiful than Russia. He spoke once of happy days in the country when he sat on the bank of the Volga at sunset and looked out over the immense fields of ripening wheat. He said he remembered one such evening, sitting with his father and his family, surrounded by friends. While they all fished in the river, Yakov's father told tales of things that had happened long before.

Only once did Stalin ever mention his half sister, Svetlana, and then fleetingly. "Malenkaia," he called her, "the little one." Once he asked me what I was going to do after the war. I told him I wanted to find my children. I said I still had two boys and a girl, but that my wife had been killed in the concentration camp at Auschwitz. He asked me if I had a picture of my family, and I showed it to him. He looked at the snapshot and became thoughtful. I then decided to risk asking him about his personal affairs.

"Have you a family?" He looked at me, hesitated, and said, "Yes, I have a wife and two children." I asked him if he would visit them immediately after his return to Russia. He replied, "Of course I will!" Then I put another question: "Lieutenant, is it true what your Russian soldiers say, that every prisoner will be punished for getting into captivity?" He paused. "Yes," he said, "it is true, but you must bear in mind that in my case I was severely wounded and was unconscious when I was taken prisoner." And after a while he added, "It was not my fault that they saved me. What could I do?" I agreed with him on this point, but I had the feeling that we were both unconvinced. Joseph Stalin's order that Russians who surrendered would be ruthlessly punished regardless of the circumstances was already known to all the Russian prisoners, and many of them were afraid to return home. Young Stalin was fully aware that his fate would not be different from that of his comrades.

Stalin was correct and friendly to his fellow prisoners, but to the German officers he was always rude, replying insultingly even to routine questions. Once, while we were having our German lesson, the door of his room opened and Colonel von Wachtmeister walked in, followed by two junior officers. Stalin jumped to his feet, furious. When the commandant asked him a simple question, instead of replying he threw himself on the bed with his back to the Germans, cursing them and making an obscene gesture. For this he was given ten days' arrest, and our lessons were temporarily discontinued.

Escape attempts were frequent in the camp. I remember an Alsatian, Lieutenant Kruger, who with another French officer somehow got hold of a German uniform and in this disguise walked out of the main gate and into the German barracks. Three months later the news filtered through that the two had reached their unit in North Africa. Another French officer, a quiet, bookish man, managed to cut his way unobtrusively through the barbed wire while the rest of the prisoners were taking their daily walk. It took him an hour to get through the fence and crawl out the other side, but he managed to find his way back to France. Others were not so lucky. One day we had a visit from the Gestapo. Instead of their usual uniform, the Gestapo men were this time in civilian clothes. They ordered us outside, stripped us, and spent the next five hours searching our quarters. After they had finished, we were ordered to return to our barracks. The Gestapo men left the camp in small groups. As they did so, seven of our officers in civilian clothes slipped through the front gate, among them Lieutenant Lebrun. The seven were all captured, executed, and their ashes returned to camp in urns to be displayed as a warning.

Another group of Polish, French, and Belgian officers had planned an escape tunnel. They dug it under Barracks 11, where Stalin and Blum were billeted, since this building was closest to the fence. Because a guard was posted there day and night, the other Germans paid little attention to the premises, and the prisoners were able to hide underneath the flooring and start their tunnel in relative safety.

The author of this article stands third from right in a group of officers imprisoned at the international camp at Lübeck. The photograph was taken before Stalin's arrival late in 1942.

Stalin knew nothing of this escape attempt going on under him, although ironically enough it would eventually cost him his life.

The tunnelers first dug a well five feet deep, and from there began to tunnel outward. Using a stolen electric motor, they built a device for hoisting earth. The work went quickly, and soon they were able to surface in a wheat field ten or fifteen yards beyond the fence. That evening, twenty-two officers disguised in civilian clothes hid under Barracks 11. At ten o'clock, on signal, the first man crawled through the tunnel and into the field, the next following him after an interval of five minutes. Three of the prisoners had already escaped through the field and down the road. The fourth, creeping through the wheat, met a tipsy German corporal on his way back to the quarters. The corporal thought at first that it was some soldier and his girl in the bushes and called out as a joke, but the other, unnerved and unfamiliar with the language, stammered that he was a prisoner-of-war officer. Immediately the sobered corporal covered him with his pistol and fired an alarm shot. Those under Barracks 11 knew then that the game was up and stayed where they were until seven o'clock the next morning, when all prisoners were allowed to move freely in the camp. They managed to sneak back to their quarters and change into uniform before roll call.

Meanwhile, the corporal had taken the escaped officer to the guardhouse, and since no one was there to interrogate him, he was locked up overnight. At roll call it was discovered that three other officers were missing. The recaptured prisoner refused to tell how he had got outside the camp, and a searching party failed to find the exit in the wheat field. Not until the following day did a sergeant, investigating on his own, finally locate it. When he crept into the tunnel, he found that it led under Stalin's barracks.

Wachtmeister was very upset because the diggers had been able to operate so freely, because the prisoner's interrogation had been delayed, and because it had taken so long to discover the tunnel. An investigation committee was coming from Berlin, and he feared a court-martial. Attempting to cover up his negligence, he announced that the tunnel had been dug from the wheat field to Barracks 11 by Lübeck communists for the purpose of rescuing Stalin. To prove it he produced a number of communist leaflets that he asserted had been found in the tunnel, and he asked to have his dangerous prisoner removed to another camp. The Berlin committee accepted the commandant's fable as fact. The next night Stalin was taken away to an unknown destination, which I later learned was Oranienburg. I never saw him again, although I did hear that his father had refused to exchange him for Field Marshal Paulus, the commander of the German army conquered at Stalingrad.

Since the war there have been conflicting stories about what happened to young Stalin after he was taken to Oranienburg. One of the more colorful recent reports maintains that he escaped from prison, had a son by an Italian woman now living in Piedmont, and fought against the Nazis as a member of an Italian partisan group. When his group was surrounded, he killed himself by holding a hand grenade to his chest.

Another account was given last year by Walter Usslepp, a former SS platoon leader at Oranienburg. According to Usslepp, Stalin was treated with consideration in the hope that he might undertake propaganda against the Soviet Union. In the spring of 1944 he was driven to a Berlin armaments factory, where he was supposed to make a speech to slave laborers and German workers denouncing Russia and communism. Instead he shouted in broken German "Stalin big—Hitler *kaputt!*"

This account would accord with the end of the story as I heard it shortly after the war, while I was attached to British 30th Corps at Lüneburg. This version came from several camp inmates and a German noncommissioned officer at Oranienburg who said that Yakov Dzhugashvili-Stalin was executed on Himmler's direct orders. The SS guards stripped him in his quarters, taped his mouth, dragged him naked into the yard, and shot him.

Michael A. Budek, LL.D. (Cracow), LL.M. (Harvard) was Major of Horse Artillery in the Polish Army. He came to the United States in 1950 and now lives in Cambridge, Massachusetts. He has been a research associate in international aviation law at the Harvard Business School and is presently interpreter and legal research assistant at the Suffolk County Superior Court in Boston.

47

The Admirable Crichton

TOMI UNGERER

James Crichton Esq.

"I have decided to be admirable, in all, for all," said Cyrano de Bergerac in Rostand's play. He spoke for the Renaissance man, whose ambitions knew no bounds; for Pico della Mirandola, that comely cavalier who proposed to defend nine hundred theses on mathematics, theology, and scholastic subjects; for Leon Battista Alberti, architect, artist, musician, author, who could tame the wildest horse and the wildest woman, and jump over a man's head from a standing start; for Leonardo himself. He spoke also for the Admirable Crichton, ill-fated Mirror of Perfection.

James Crichton was born on August 19, 1560, in Dumfriesshire. He was the son of Robert Crichton, who became Lord Advocate of Scotland. A prodigy, the boy entered St. Andrews University at ten, and received his B.A. at twelve (or thirteen), his M.A. two years later. He must have spent the next few years in raging

study and self-cultivation, for we soon find him in possession of twelve languages, of the profundities of scholarship, and of uncommon athletic skill and courtly grace. He was aided in his intellectual pursuits by an extraordinary memory. He could repeat verbatim anything he had ever read, could even, on demand, recite verse backward. He is described as tall, handsome, blond, blue-eyed, trimly bearded. At some time in his troubled teens he quarreled with his father about religion and was ordered out of Scotland. He went to France and served in the army.

Now fact takes on the adornments of fancy. Many of the adornments are supplied by his fantastic biographer, Sir Thomas Urquhart, who made the ever memorable translation of Rabelais, who contrived a universal language in which every word could be read backward or forward, and who, it is said, died of a fit of laughter on learning that King Charles II of England was restored to his throne.

According to Sir Thomas, Crichton posted notices throughout Paris, challenging all comers to dispute with him on a certain day on any science, liberal art, or discipline, whether metaphysical, arithmetical, geometrical, astronomical, musical, optical, cosmographical, trigonometrical, or statistical, whether in Hebrew, Syriac, Arabic, Greek, Latin, Spanish, French, Italian, English, Dutch, Flemish, or Slavonian, in verse or prose at the disputant's choice. All the rarest minds of Paris set themselves to prepare pitfalls for the overweening challenger. "All this while, the Admirable Scot (for so from henceforth he was called) minding more his hawking, hunting, tilting, vaulting, riding of well-managed horses, tossing of the pike . . . flourishing of colors, dancing, fencing, swimming, jumping, throwing of the bar, playing at the tennis, balloon, or long-catch . . . playing at the chess, billiards, troumadame, and other suchlike chambersports, singing, playing on the lute

and other musical instruments, masking, balling, reveling, and . . . being more addicted to and plying closer the courting of handsome ladies and a jovial cup in the company of bacchanalian blades than . . ." (Sir Thomas extricates himself from his sentence a page further on.)

On the appointed day the rector of the university gave the word to his learned champions to "fall on." They argued of everything knowable, *de omni scibili*, but the incomparable Crichton confounded them all "and publicly evidenced such an universality of knowledge and accurate promptness in resolving of doubts, distinguishing of obscurities, expressing the members of a distinction in adequate terms of art . . . [that] with all excogitable variety of learning . . . [he] entertained . . . the nimble-witted Parisians from nine o'clock in the morning till six at night." The rector then favored him with a panegyric speech of half an hour's continuance and presented him with a diamond ring and a purse of gold. "There was so great a plaudite in the school, such a humming and clapping of hands, that all the concavities of the colleges thereabout did resound with the echo of the noise thereof." The next day, to refresh his brains, he went to the Louvre and gave an exhibition of horsemanship, picking off the ring with his lance fifteen times in succession.

Unfortunately, no one so far has discovered any corroboration of this great joust of erudition, wit, and dexterity. No doubt the silence of the Parisian pundits is due to shame.

There is, however, no question that Crichton appeared in Genoa, destitute, in July, 1579. He addressed the senate in a Latin speech, which was published. But as the businesslike Genoese proffered no gold-filled purses, he pushed on to Venice. The records of the ruling Council of Ten report, on August 19, 1580, the arrival of James Crichton, Scottish noble of rare and singular attainments. He gave a public extempore Latin

By MORRIS BISHOP

oration and "filled the minds of all with astonishment and stupor." The Council gratified him with one hundred gold crowns, a handsome lecture fee in any era. Various testimonies refer to him as a monster of learning, a miracle of perfection whose only peer was Alexander the Great; he outdid the learned in learning, the gallants in notable seductions. A printed handbill, which perhaps he prompted, calls him a prodigy of prodigies, who has Aristotle and the commentators at his fingers' ends and Thomas Aquinas and Duns Scotus by heart. The handbill says that he has disputed with the Greeks on the procession of the Holy Ghost. And now he has retired to a villa to prepare two thousand propositions, which he will defend in the church of St. John and St. Paul in two months' time.

Crichton's charm subjugated Aldus Manutius the second, the famous Venetian scholar-printer who had begun publishing at nine. Aldus dedicated to Crichton his *Paradoxa Ciceronis*, with a high-flown liminary epistle reporting that Crichton had revealed the errors of Aristotle in a three-day orgy of scholarship, answering his opponents either by logical and ordinary methods or by the secret devices of astronomy or in mathematical, poetic, and other forms, at their choice. People thronged to his exhibitions as they had to hear Plato when he debarked from Sicily and emptied the stands at the Olympic Games.

(The proposal of theses and their defense as a sporting event were a feature of medieval scholasticism; the announcement that Abelard would take on all comers could fill a cathedral. The Renaissance exaggerated, as was its wont. Crichton's contemporary Giacomo Mazzoni proposed to defend 5,197 propositions on Aristotle and Plato. Luther's 95 theses tacked on the door of the Wittenberg church were a mere trifle. The scholarly challenge, which has dwindled to angry "Letters to the Editor," would perhaps be worth reviving.)

After an unfruitful stay in Padua, where he delivered an extempore oration in praise of ignorance, as if "to reconcile his audience to their comparative inferiority," Crichton moved to Mantua. The city and territory were ruled by the old, bigoted Duke Guglielmo Gonzaga; his son and heir, Vincenzo, just twenty, was a bully, bravo, and lecher in the Renaissance tradition, and the terror of the city.

According to Sir Thomas Urquhart, my unreliable darling, Crichton challenged and defeated a swaggering furioso, spitting him neatly so as to describe a perfect isosceles triangle on his breast. Further, says Sir Thomas, Crichton produced a play of his own for the carnival. He took all fifteen parts in a performance that lasted five hours. One of the maids of honor ruptured a vein laughing. And he won the favors of a lady besought by Prince Vincenzo. The love scene is majestic, though verging on the indelicate: ". . . the visuriency of either, by ushering the tacturiency of both, made the attrectation of both consequent to the inspection of either: here it was that Passion was active, and Action passive; they both being overcome by other, and each the conqueror. To speak of her *hirquitalliency* at the *elevation* of the *pole* of his Microcosm, or of his luxuriousness to erect a *gnomon* on her *horizontal* dial, will perhaps be held by some to be expressions of obsceneness, and offensive to the purity of chaste ears."

According to Sir Thomas, Crichton was interrupted in his dalliance by the jealous Prince Vincenzo. It is possible; but we had best abandon Sir Thomas for the inquest on the subsequent events. The prince testified that at one in the morning he was taking the fresh air with a companion. Mistaking a hooded passerby for a friend, he jostled him in jest and brought him to the ground. The figure, Crichton, rose and stabbed the prince's companion in the back. The prince engaged Crichton and delivered a happy thrust. Crichton, recognizing royalty,

begged his pardon and died, as did the prince's companion.

Duke Guglielmo was furious at the loss of a man "famous throughout the world." The prince was officially cleared of blame, but the city and the courts of Italy continued to talk. The prince was the only living witness, and his word was little esteemed. He was normally no match for Crichton, and his sword was a span shorter than his adversary's. The story went that Crichton, on recognizing his superior, had knelt and proffered his sword by the blade, and that the prince had seized it and run him through. Five years later—such is the consistency of human behavior—the prince and two archers disturbed the amours of the organist of the castle basilica and wounded him. The victim named the archers, and the prince abandoned them to justice.

At any rate, the Admirable Crichton was dead at twenty-two, with his promise unfulfilled. A picture was disseminated, showing him on horseback with a lance in one hand and a book in the other, a posture equally inapt for reading or fighting. The picture, unhappily, has not survived.

Shall we mourn his early disappearance? Various encomia call him the glory and ornament of Parnassus, the phoenix of nature, a shining particle of divine mind and majesty. On the other hand his extant Latin poems offer no great reward. Scaliger says, *"Il était un peu fat"* (a bit of a coxcomb); he was more worthy of wonder than of love. The scholar Boccalini asserts that while Crichton astonished the vulgar, he nauseated the wise by his pretensions.

He has left us, at least, an ideal of universal accomplishment, and he has left us a phrase: "the Admirable Crichton." To leave a phrase—that is a rare and splendid legacy.

Morris Bishop's most recent contributions to Horizon *have been "1066" for the Autumn, 1966, issue and the "Letters of Petrarch" for Winter, 1967.*

MUST THE ARTIST REBEL?
(Ask the Greeks.)

The first named artists in history produced their works
of genius under conditions that,
we have been told a million times over, can only stifle art

By M. I. FINLEY

In 468 B.C., Hiero I, tyrant of Syracuse in Sicily, finally succeeded in gaining the most sought after of Greek athletic prizes, victory in the four-horse chariot race at the Olympic Games. The poet Pindar expected to be given the commission to write the victory ode, but the tyrant appointed Pindar's competitor Bacchylides instead. Pindar poured out his anger in an ode he wrote anyway, railing against his fate and throwing a few barbs at Bacchylides along the way—"See, the ape to children is a pretty thing, pretty indeed." But he knew his place and he cautioned himself: "My necessity/is to escape the teeth of reproach for excessive blame./ Standing afar, I saw Archilochus the scold,/laboring helpless and fattening on his own cantankerous/hate, naught else; prosperity, blessed with fortune, gives the highest wisdom."*

An old story that, of vendettas among poets and artists and of treacherous relations with patrons. The Greek variant is especially interesting because it was the first in history (at least in the West) and because it underwent some illuminating and paradoxical transformations in the course of several centuries. When Pindar had his quarrel with Hiero, his kind of poetry and Hiero's kind of tyranny were both dying out. The self-governing community, either democratic or oligarchic in its political structure, was becoming the rule in the Greek world, and the community itself was displacing individual tyrants and aristocrats as the great patron of the arts. In this new, community context the Greek experience is a test case of the tensions between the artist and his society, of how an equilibrium may be successfully achieved; and that problem, after all, is still very much with us.

The Greek story is the first, simply because the Greek artist was the first to emerge as a recognizable, self-conscious individual. No doubt the men who built the pyramids and temples in Egypt and conceived the palaces and statues in Babylonia were also individuals. But they remain totally anonymous; even their work lacks the hallmark of individual personalities. However "Archilochus the scold," who flourished about 650 B.C. on the Aegean island of Paros, and even earlier the poet Hesiod from Boeotia on the mainland of Greece, were already identifiable not only as the authors of certain specific works but also in their themes—in the way they wrote and thought and felt. By the next century potters and sculptors were regularly signing their works, and they, like the poets who specialized in choral odes, actively competed for commissions, sometimes traveling considerable distances, as Pindar did, going from his native Boeotia as far as Sicily (then a largely Greek island) when there was work to be done and paid for.

By Pindar's time the Greeks were widely dispersed around the shores of the Mediterranean, but the *polis* (conventionally translated "city-state") remained the focus of political and social life. Within Hellas there were perhaps fifteen hundred more or less

* From *The Odes of Pindar* translated by Richmond Lattimore, © 1947 by U. of Chicago Press.

A fourth-century B.C. *Greek vase depicts Heracles, right, watching his own statue being painted*

independent units. Athens was much the largest, with a territory of one thousand square miles and a population at its peak of perhaps two hundred and fifty thousand, including the slaves as well as the freeborn. Possibly another dozen communities exceeded forty thousand; the majority counted their inhabitants in the few thousands.

The Greeks were thus in a permanent face-to-face relationship within their communities, and given the size of the ordinary *polis*, most citizens knew each other personally, so that their political life was also an intimate one. Thanks to the Mediterranean climate, furthermore, much of their social and political activity could be carried on in the open. They met to talk and argue in the town square, the agora; they held their political assemblies in the open; even their theatres were open-air auditoriums, and their most important religious ceremonials took place out of doors.

All this had a direct bearing on Greek art and artists, as did such social institutions as slavery. If manual labor was the lot of the slave, the free man could not look upon such labor as a vocation or a social good in itself, even if he were compelled by necessity to do it. One consequence of this attitude toward manual labor was a subtle distinction between the literary and the visual arts. There were no slave poets or dramatists, but there were many slave potters, stonemasons, and gem engravers. Some of the latter turned out work of the highest quality, so high that it is absolutely impossible to tell from the finished product whether a vase or carving is to be attributed to a slave or a free craftsman. There is a simple way that every visitor to Athens can test this for himself. He need only look closely at the magnificently carved moldings or the fluting of the columns of the Erechtheum on the Acropolis and try to draw distinctions. He will find it impossible to do so, yet we happen to know by the chance survival of fragments of the building accounts that some of the most delicate operations on this particular temple were per-formed by slaves—and in the final stages of the construction period, when the opportunities to cause damage were greatest. We also know that at the highest levels, among the great sculptors such as Phidias or Praxiteles or among the architects, there were no slaves. Nevertheless, even these men of genius, highly reputed, praised, and sought after, were looked upon as remarkable craftsmen, not to be classed with the great poets. There was much curiosity and discussion among the Greeks about the nature of poetic inspiration, but none about painters or sculptors, because their skill was widely shared, by slaves as well as free men; the difference was only one of degree, whereas the poet was set apart by a difference in kind. A modern authority has put the point very neatly: "only the tongue was inspired by the gods, never the hand." One reason the Greeks had no word for art or artist is that they could not have conceived of a single word to cover the whole range of the artist's creative activities.

The vigorous bald-headed man with upraised arms above may be Phidias sculptured by himself. The figure appears on a reduced copy of the shield that Phidias made for his statue (since lost) of Athena. According to Plutarch, the sculptor inserted himself in this mythological scene of war between Greeks and Amazons.

The choice of the word "tongue" is exact. Although most Greeks seem to have been literate, their culture was an oral one to an astonishing degree. Its perfect architectural symbol is that most characteristic of all Greek structures, the stoa, or roofed colonnaded walk, where men could stroll and talk, protected from the hot summer sun and the heavy rains of spring and autumn. The important philosophical school called Stoicism took its name from the fact that its founder, Zeno, came to Athens in 313 B.C. and soon began to teach in the so-called Painted Stoa, built during the fifth century B.C. on the northwestern boundary of the agora. A century before Zeno, Socrates also "taught" in and about the Athenian agora, and his reputation rests on a lifetime of talk, for he never wrote a line.

Plutarch tells a revealing story about the Athenian soldiers and sailors who were captured after the failure of their expedition to Sicily in 413 B.C. Seven thousand of them were flung into the abandoned quarries in Syracuse and left there to die. Some, however, were set free because they could recite by heart choruses from the tragedies of Euripides; "for the Sicilians, it seems, had a passion for his poetry greater than that of any other Hellenes outside Greece." The story may not be true, but that doesn't really matter: it rests on important and indisputable facts of Greek culture. One was the remarkable way it held together despite the great dispersion and the political fragmentation of the Greeks. Another was the almost total reliance on oral communication and memory. Plato, himself a prolific writer of magnificent prose, expressed open distrust of books. They could not be questioned the way a teacher could, and besides they weakened the memory. For every Greek who read an ode of Pindar's or a play by Euripides, there were thousands who knew them solely from hearing them. Had there been enough copies of Euripides's plays in circulation, the Syracusans would have been less eager to hear the memorized snatches known to the Athenian prisoners.

These prisoners were not professional soldiers. They were ordinary Athenians, giving military service when called upon. That some knew by heart choruses of Euripides, a contemporary playwright, is itself very revealing. They would not have learned them in school, as they might have learned the verses of Homer, but in the theatre or informally. The Theatre of Dionysus on the southern slope of the Acropolis, where the tragedies were performed, had room for some fourteen thousand people. At the annual five-day spring festival called the Great Dionysia, in which choral odes and comedies had their place as well as tragedies, more than a thousand men and boys took part in the choruses, the acting, and the music-making.

Today the tragedies of Aeschylus, Sophocles, and Euripides are an esoteric taste, even in translation. In their own day they clearly were not, and it is not sufficient to object to this as an unfair comparison on the ground that today they are essentially the products of a long-dead civilization. The plays were not "easy" for their less educated contemporaries either, and that raises a fundamental question. Greek society was a stratified one. Apart from the slaves, there were sharp divisions (and often conflicts) among the citizens based on wealth, birth, class, and education. Were there no corresponding divergences and conflicts in taste? Of course there were. Not everyone went to the Great Dionysia, and of those who did, some went for social reasons and were bored stiff; others enjoyed the pageantry of the costumes and the settings and the music (lost to us), and they allowed the words and their meaning to pass them by; still others followed the dramatist's every nuance with the closest concentration, then went home and thought about what they had seen and perhaps argued about it. In one of his plays, *Medea*, Euripides briefly but unambiguously challenged a favorite doctrine of Socrates, and eventually Plato in turn replied to Euripides in a dialogue. Presumably there were many who heard *Medea* in the theatre who did not catch what was going on.

And yet there is a profound sense in which one may say that, unlike modern Western culture, that of the Greeks crossed all social lines and appealed to all brows, high, low, or middle. Not many captured GI's, after all, would have won their freedom if the price had been quotations from memory of the verses of T. S. Eliot or Robert Lowell—or anyone else one prefers to consider a fair modern counterpart of Euripides; but there *is* no counterpart, and that is the nub of the matter. Euripides could not write for the Theatre of Dionysus as Shakespeare wrote for the Globe, because the former came to life only on festival occasions and was otherwise an empty shell. One could not go to see a play in Athens or listen to music when one wished, but only when there was an appropriate public or community occasion, which was rare. The occasion was normally community sponsored and community organized, just as sculpture and painting were normally to be found in public buildings or in appropriate public outdoor places rather than in private houses. Not only was most art created under patronage, as it has often been, but the chief patron was the community itself, as it has rarely been, and the Greek community was no impersonal nation-state but a small, face-to-face city-state.

The relation between patron and artist has always been filled with tension: witness Pindar and Hiero. When the patron is the whole community, one expects the difficulties to be multiplied. One expects factional interests to apply pressures for or against in-

dividuals or points of view, to dominate and often to crush the artist. By and large, however, the Greek artist was able to strike a balance between the demands and the values of a community on the one hand and his own individual personality and inspiration on the other, without either sinking into anonymity and stereotyped repetitiveness or being driven to Pop Art in its pejorative sense of seeking to appeal to the lowest and broadest level of taste and sensibility. The Greek artist was neither rebel nor bohemian nor avant-gardist. He accepted his role as spokesman for his society and with it the place of art as an activity useful to the community. This is the primary reason why there were no words in Greek to express the general concepts of art and artist. In a sense, neither existed. A man wrote poetry to celebrate a wedding or an athletic victory or a military triumph; or he produced statuary to adorn temples or other public buildings, or, in Athens, graves. He did none of these things merely to "express himself," nor in the hope that someone might want to purchase them, though he exercised all the skill at his command to do them beautifully. Nietzsche once exclaimed: "They are applauding; what nonsense have I been talking?" Nothing could be more opposed to the Greek view. And the same principle held good for the minor arts; goods were produced primarily for private consumption. Greeks liked to own beautiful water jugs, cosmetic jars, necklaces, rings, even coins. But these were all objects of utility, not *objets d'art*. The home was not a museum. Indeed, the museum did not exist in their world.

How successful the Greek artists were is immediately apparent from a visit to the physical remains of their work in Greece and Sicily or to almost any large museum anywhere in the world. Their literature and their visual arts not only outlived their own civilization but continued to stimulate

and enrich the arts of later ages to a degree that probably has no parallel. The very idea of drama, of theatre as we know it, was a Greek invention of the late sixth century B.C., and within a very few years it blossomed into the powerful art of the Athenian tragedians. The nude, in Sir Kenneth Clark's words, "is an art form invented by the Greeks." Even the human statue and the column-framed temple may fairly rank as Greek inventions, for although the prototypes may have been borrowed, the final products were essentially new and original. In sum, the Greek artists produced great art (as we would call it) under conditions that, we have been told a million times over, can only stifle art and destroy it. Neither the dramatist nor the lyric poet nor the architect nor the sculptor in Greece was "free" in the romantic or post-romantic sense. Yet he seems not to have been much stifled, and he was certainly not destroyed as an artist.

For a modern viewer the situation becomes particularly difficult because of the unfamiliar way in which religion tended to touch the artist's work. For one thing, there was among the Greeks no organized church or priesthood and therefore no concept of a separation between church and state. Although there was private religious ritual in every home and in numerous private cult associations, all the major ceremonials and festivals were a state activity. In the second place, Greek polytheism retained an anthropomorphic strain. Despite the growing protests of moralists and philosophers, for most men the gods did not wholly shed the manlike qualities so nobly portrayed in the Homeric poems on which every Greek was nurtured. Perhaps the best example is provided by the archaic statues in marble and bronze of young nude males, called *kouroi* by modern art historians. More than two hundred are now known, ranging in date from about 650 to about 460 B.C., and in our museums they are sometimes labeled "Apollo" and sometimes "Youth." From the statue itself it is impossible to tell which is right, and only external evidence can decide: if the statue is known to be a funerary monument, for example, or if the base survives with an inscribed text.

The Greeks feared their gods (or at least some of them), and they placated them, chiefly through sacrifice. But they also celebrated them, and in so doing they were celebrating the divine in themselves. That is why they found it appropriate to include in religious festivals not only processions carrying the sacred image and singing hymns, but also contests in prowess and athletic skill and in the various literary and musical arts—but not, characteristically, in the plastic arts. The great craftsmen (whom we call artists) were invited to celebrate in their own way, by constructing beautiful temples adorned with sculptured friezes and pediments; by shaping statues of the god or goddess to whom the temple belonged; by building fine stadia and theatres for the contests. What went on within these sacred edifices, however, never departed from the originally aristocratic values to the extent of allowing the craftsmen to compete for prizes along with athletes and men with inspired tongues. It is no accident, finally, that the greatest of all the games were held at Olympia and Delphi, the two greatest of all Panhellenic shrines.

This "confusion" between the human and the divine helps to explain the idealized quality of so much Greek sculpture and architecture, the search for harmony and just proportion. The Greeks came to believe that the road to the ideal lay through mathematical proportions, that number was the key to harmony; so that much of the history of both architecture and sculpture can be written in mathematical terms. There were established ratios within the various elements of the human figure, as there were for the

two main perpendicular lines: one from nipple to nipple, the other the length of the torso. The Doric temple is made up of carefully considered ratios—that, for example, between the height of the columns and the distances between their axes. Within each order, Doric or Ionic, there was an essential sameness about temples for centuries on end, wherever in the Greek world they were built. Even pottery had this canonical quality; a relatively small number of shapes, each established as appropriate for a container of a certain function, were retained for centuries, until one has the illusion that the shape itself has an objective existence. Both the artist and his client knew beforehand what would come out when a temple was to be built, a statue of a victorious athlete to be cast in bronze, or a prize water jug to be thrown, fired, and painted. On neither side was there the restless search and demand for something new, something original and different.

Yet to leave it at that would be to draw a caricature of Greek art. It can be shown that not a single major line in the Parthenon is absolutely straight, that its spacings are often not quite equal. With these deliberate "distortions" the architect Ictinus created the greatest of all Doric temples. The history of the *kouroi* is still more striking. Beginning as very stiff, depersonalized figures, in which the actual human proportions are falsely reproduced, they were slowly transformed by subtle changes in the balances and the ratios, until an unnamed sculptor, shortly before 480 B.C., produced a marble in Athens, just under three feet high, that Sir Kenneth Clark has singled out as "the perfect human body . . . the first beautiful nude in art." The architects and sculptors accepted the authority of the community and the canons that had been established and worked within them. Yet they were not driven to stultifying monotony. Within the imposed limits they explored all the possibilities fully

The commanding full-length figure of a dramatist, above, is thought to be Euripides. A rebel in the arts, he was nonetheless a citizen first and foremost, speaking to and for his fellow Athenians.

and freely, bringing their skills, their imagination and inventiveness, to play in every detail. Individual genius found its outlet in nuances rather than in radical innovation.

In the literary field tragedy, which was linked just as closely with religion and the festivals, shows similar development. We take the drama so much for granted that it requires a feat of the imagination to appreciate that the idea itself is not a "natural" one, that it had to be invented, speaking quite literally. The inventor, according to a tradition that is probably reliable, was an Athenian named Thespis, who flourished in the latter part of the sixth century B.C. More accurately, he was what the Renaissance would have called the "first inventor," for it was Aeschylus, in the next generation, who transformed Thespis's embryo by the simple device of adding a second actor to the cast of chorus and one actor. Tragedy then had a history in Athens of about two hundred years, during which the formal rules were little altered beyond the addition of a third actor. Again it is a story of artists working within an accepted framework and producing a remarkable variety of fresh and enduring works.

Most tragedies were written for the early spring festival in Athens, the Great Dionysia. The third, fourth, and fifth days were assigned to tragedy, each day to a single playwright who wrote for the occasion three tragedies (we would call them one-act poetic plays) and also a grotesque "satyr-play." The occasion was a solemn one, and the writers were fully conscious of all its implications. Since they were Greeks, that did not bind them to religious themes in the narrow sense, but it frequently turned them to the traditional myths for their stories; and it required them to concentrate on the most fundamental questions of human existence, of man's behavior and destiny under divine power and authority. They, too, followed the formal canons of language

and meter, of theme and structure, without suffering stultification. With Euripides we reach a remarkable level of freedom in the way he probed the traditional myths and questioned the most hallowed beliefs, such as his hints that slaves were human or his undisguised concern with the corruption of power. Euripides must have cut uncomfortably close to the bone for many in his audience—witness the persistent gibing at him in the comedies of Aristophanes—yet he was never suppressed or boycotted. And it was Euripides about whom Plutarch told the story of the Athenian prisoners in Sicily.

Aristophanes and the other writers of comedy also enjoyed an astonishing degree of freedom at religious festivals: they sneered and joked in the most boisterous and offensive way at everything from the gods to the politicians to the political institutions and the people themselves. The acme of this freedom came in the opening decade of the long and decisive war between Athens and Sparta, during which Aristophanes (and no doubt other playwrights) went far beyond what any contemporary state would conceivably tolerate in his jokes about the war effort. In *The Acharnians*, for example, one of his earliest plays, the long closing scene is a riotous piece of buffoonery in which the leading character abates the evil of war by making his own peace with the enemy.

Only a very self-confident community could have permitted that, and in this instance it was not only a matter of permission and toleration; it was also one of active support in the production. But by the end of Aristophanes's career something seems to have been lost. His later plays no longer have named or identifiable people as their characters, and after him comedy quickly turned away from the great political and social themes and from the hard-hitting tone. It became a comedy of manners built on

monotonous, conventionalized plots, respectable and safe in its moralizing on the virtue-triumphant theme. The conclusion is hard to avoid that this so-called New Comedy was appropriate to the new political situation.

By the closing decades of the fourth century B.C. the classical Greek city-state had come to an end as an independent political entity, to be replaced by new tyrannies and new monarchical forms of government. The history of Greek art also entered a new phase, of which the personal portrait in sculpture, replacing the ideal types of the earlier phase, is the adequate symbol. Not even the gods and heroes were immune. The Aphrodites of the new age are women who feel shame and love, who are unmistakable individuals in a way that no classical statue ever was. And in Alexandria, the Greek metropolis founded in Egypt by Alexander the Great, the first museum was built. The *objet d'art* had been invented.

It is a commonplace that the relationship between the artist and his public is a two-way one, but it is no less true for being overfamiliar. The artists of ancient Greece demonstrated beyond any possibility of doubt that it is possible to produce great art without rejecting or rebelling against the basic values of the community for whom and to whom the artist speaks. Our world seems to have lost that balance to a large extent. It is fashionable to put the blame entirely on the artists and their claims to a higher truth. But a two-way relationship requires participation on both sides, and it is fair to suggest that if the artist finds himself unable to function as his Greek predecessors did, part of the trouble may lie in society itself.

M. I. Finley is Reader in Ancient Social and Economic History at Cambridge University. His most recent article for Horizon *was a reconsideration of the Trojan War. It appeared in the Spring, 1967, issue.*

On Polyphony and a

It has come to our attention that a certain musical ensemble, called the Beatles, has been gaining popularity in this

Revolutions tend to be rather arbitrary in their choice of agents and instruments. Have you heard the dreadful story of the thumb, with which the terrible Count Orlov is said to have throttled the czar of Russia, Peter III, by suddenly pressing his windpipe while he was drinking? And now the Beatles have come on with their own particular revolution, of which their thumbs, and indeed windpipes, are the chief instrumentality. A revolution in music, hence in movement, rhythm, communication: "the revolution of the sexy lamb" that Allen Ginsberg foretold in 1959, three years before the advent of the Beatles, when he was but a voice in the wilderness of the *Times Lit. Sup.*

The Beatles are four young men* in Beethoven haircuts, whose social significance as a group is far out of proportion to their numbers. They are strummers of guitars, pounders of drums, singers of songs, and the most influential composers of our time. Though none of them can blow piano like Monk or sing like Caruso, their microgroove records laid edge to edge stretch from the London Festival Hall to the Avalon Ballroom in San Francisco. Not only their poetry but their very accents have been graven indelibly in the narrow margins of our *Zeitgeist:* "Ooooh, O-oooh, I wanna hole Jo-han," etc.

"I think we are getting influenced now by ourselves more and more," one of them said not long ago, regretting the circumstance that there was no one else left to look up to. "Think of us as idols . . ." But success is as necessary to the Beatles as failure was to Mozart; their whole performance as pathfinders and mind-blowers depends on this extraordinary power to sway the multitudes, seemingly forever. When *Beatles: The Men who Freed Music* is written, it will be the story of how a whole society—not otherwise noted for its generosity to poets—has subsidized its creative subconscious to the tune of twenty million dollars a year.

What makes this situation so interesting musically is that the Beatles are now in a position to do anything at all and have it listened to. Their recent *oeuvre*, notably *Sgt. Pepper's Lonely Hearts Club Band* and the *Magical Mystery Tour*, is a great eclectic circus of Indian raga, Salvation Army, Benjamin British, tailgate, gutbucket, and aleatoric chance-music, all handled without hang-ups or uptightness. There is a lovely lawlessness about it that reminds one of the "indeterminacy" experiments of John Cage, the father of random music-making. Cage did this sort of thing for years, but he had to explain himself. The Beatles do it without explaining: "You don't say love, you do it" is an old psychedelic proverb.

If this seems like too much of a mélange, it was obviously ordained that way. The Beatles were born on the cusp, as astrologers say, where two spheres of influence come together; in this case the signs of Memphis rock and London music hall. The very name of the group suggests a Kafka bag of men turning to metamorphosis, and for that matter the French word *béatilles* used to be defined as "all kinds of ingredients, that may be fancied, for to put together into a pie, or otherwise, viz. Cock's combes, stones, or kidnies, sweetbreads of veal, mushrums, bottoms of hartichocks, etc." Under the circumstances, it was inevitable that the Beatles should emerge as the great syncretists and mixmasters of our day.

When they first appeared on the scene six years ago, they sang like very young and energetic angels flapping wing-shaped guitars, with a sound already remarkable for its dark timbre and strong basses. In striking contrast to the steel edge of their playing was the fuzzy quality of their singing: those hooded consonants and stubby vowels that were the result, ecologically, of generations of Liverpool adenoids enlarged by Mersey dews and damps. Rhythmically these early Beatle numbers were lineal descendants of "race records," Mississippi blues, Alabama field hollers, and such. But while the thumb was playing with blues tension, the windpipe was enunciating British sentiments closer to Bea Lillie than Lead Belly. The words were surprisingly bland, coming from a generation whose mod/rocker antics were just then making headlines and whose taste for unabated high volume was blowing the roof off the discotheques.

Apparently the Beatles had got to the root of some secret sorrow and made it articulate: the first groping love efforts of a generation that had undergone the trauma of permissive parenthood and demand feeding. Beneath the tough-sounding surface of

* Names furnished on request

56   *By* FREDERIC V. GRUNFELD

New Vocal Quartet

this music one could detect a vaguely oedipal predicament: Don't be bad to me; Hold me love me; I call your name but you're not there; I'm a loser; Did you have to treat me oh so bad? These are clearly songs of innocence rather than experience, and when Lennon and McCartney ask, "Don't go 'way I'm afraid that I might miss you," they touch on the same anguish that an earlier British poet summed up so poignantly in the line: "You must *never* go down to the end of the town without consulting me."

What had begun as an *art brut,* all capitals and no lower case, gradually acquired more subtle shades of pop impressionism. As the focus shifted from second-person accusative to third-person feminine ("She's a Woman"), the melodies stopped coming down with a bump on the hard beats, and the sound of guitar-percussion was augmented with cowbells, tambourines, and the electric organ.

In "We Can Work It Out" echoes of a French musette band broke like a thunderclap across a pop scene that had heard nothing but four-four time for fifty years; the Beatles had independently invented waltz time, here disguised as triplets, and even this simple rhythmic innovation shook the pop world to its foundations.

These were the Beatles' *Wanderjahre,* and though their efforts to shore up the British pound took them as far west as Texas and California, their whole style was moving further and further toward the East. George Harrison (afterward to spend a semester in India with Ravi Shankar) took up the uncertain sitar that is to be heard twanging for the first time in

"Norwegian Wood." It was a decisive addition to the arsenal of Beatle sounds. In time, after some other experiments with Indian ragas and gurus, the Beatles found their real depth as the mind-expanding dragomans of the love generation, translating Yoga into pop and interpreting the new Vedanta for the Western scene.

Their poetry loses its shrill note of sexual urgency and goes softly out of focus: "We all live in a yellow submarine, yellow submarine..." The *Revolver* album, with its striking *nouveau*-Rorschach cover by Klaus Voorman, stakes out the boundaries of the Beatles' expanded domain, now no longer circumscribed by the Mersey beat. "Taxman," the opening song in the album, offers a first attempt at social protest for people in the upper income brackets: "If you get too cold I'll tax the heat, If you take a walk I'll tax your feet." "Good Day Sunshine" revives the spirit of barrelhouse and barbershop; "For No One" borrows a romantic French horn obbligato from Schubert's *Hirt auf dem Felsen.* Though love appeals are more casual than ever—"I'll make love to you if you want me to"—the group is not above reverting to an old-fashioned crooner ballad, intoned so beatifically that butter wouldn't melt in their guitars. Harrison's sitar, improving with practice, appears in "Love You To" and "Tomorrow Never Knows," proclaiming a new-found doctrine of flower power: "Turn off your mind, relax and float downstream," at which point the sound does become very relaxed and unpremeditated, close to the edge of indeterminacy. But the album's real *pièce*

de résistance, "Eleanor Rigby," is actually a kind of Lennon - McCartney passion chorale:

Eleanor Rigby
Picks up the rice in the church
Where a wedding has been,
Lives in a dream
Waits at the window
Wearing the face that she keeps in a jar
by the door,
Who is it for?
All the lonely people, where do they all
come from?
All the lonely people, where do they all
belong?

In the outline and texture of its string accompaniment "Eleanor Rigby" bears a more than fleeting resemblance to the *Bachianas Brasileiras* of Villa-Lobos. "I don't like that kind of classical music. I can't stand it," McCartney explained to the underground press afterward. "It's all things like that that I just don't like, but I see how I can use them. 'Eleanor Rigby'—if it had been anything else I think it would have been a real mess, having the violins like that on there, having it arranged in that sort of way. But it fitted, it was just lucky that it fitted. I think I like that kind of sound of things, but I haven't got an LP like that, that I like. I've got LP's like that, but I never put them on."

Intentionally or not, the Beatles had already breached the wall between "that kind" of classical music—passé, insuperable—and whatever it was they had

been doing. With their next single they arrived at virtually the same intersection between the square and the amoebic that Kurt Weill had reached, for some brief but glorious moments, in his Berlin theatre songs of the 1920's. "Penny Lane" opens up neobaroque vistas, with Bach trumpets blowing hallelujahs for the fireman who "likes to keep his fire engine clean, it's a clean machine." And "Strawberry Fields Forever," on the other side, completes the job of utterly demolishing the form and formula of the erstwhile "pop single." Rhythmically this is the stickiest wicket yet: "no-thing is real [in triplets] and no-thing to get hung a-bout [in four-four time]" followed by measures of two-four, six-eight, nine-eight, and back to four-four, like Stravinsky's *Sacre du Printemps*.

Even if this were all a giant put-on, as there was reason to suspect, and they were wearing their tongue in the cheek that they kept by the microphone, the Beatles' faithful audience of flower people was perfectly willing to go along. A put-on, whatever its intentions, is merely that higher form of truth that Dr. Freud recognized long ago as an instrument of revolution—"Humor is not resigned; it is rebellious..." Cavorting together in the midst of this imaginary landscape are the chaste unicorn of poets and Ginsberg's sexy lamb.

The Beatles have come to the point where the message has outgrown the medium. *Sgt. Pepper* contrives to be a sort of play within a play, à la Brecht, with the Beatles already at one remove from their former cherubic selves. Indeed, the cover shows them and a quartet of wax dummies of themselves from Madame Tussaud's, looking on at their own symbolic funeral. Musically it is all done with mirrors—the happiest orgy of free association since Wagner invented his ninety leitmotifs: jangling harps and harpsichords, wheezing accordions, the gatling-gun rhythms of the Tamla-Motown Detriot Negro style, Caliban thumping a

high-hat, electric guitars going off like wobbly oboes, a choral *fugato* on "We shall scrimp and save," dogs barking, cocks crowing, paeans to a "Mr. K" who could be Kafka or Klee, memories of Fred and Adele Astaire, a charge of light brigades and an instant-gamaka Hindu chant about saving the world through love. As usual the libretto is illumined by flashes of brilliant psychological insight. Certainly the Beatle lines, "Will you still need me / Will you still feed me / When I'm sixty-four," are a more penetrating utterance on the subject than "Let me not to the marriage of true minds/Admit impediments." And the final song in the album belongs to the great pessimist tradition of Villon's Belle Heaulmière or T. S. Eliot's Prufrock wearing the bottoms of their trousers rolled:

> I read the news today oh boy
> About a lucky man who
> made the grade . . .
> He blew his mind out in a car
> He didn't notice that the
> lights had changed

A forty-one-man orchestra, only slightly smaller than the one Mahler used for the Symphony of a Thousand, raises a vast banshee wail at the news; if only Edgar Varèse had lived to hear that sound emanating from a jukebox! It glides to a stop with the note on which the world will end, the most definitive final chord in the history of music; it alone is worth the price of admission. Nobody else, not even Rachmaninoff, ever carried off a *Schluss Akkord* with such panache.

Hard on its heels came another bacchanal, the "All You Need is Love" single, which turned out to be the national anthem of psychedelia. Underscoring its revolutionary character is a quote from the Marseillaise, but those martial strains lead into a chant of "love, love, love," interwoven with tidings of goodwill:

Nothing you can know that isn't known
Nothing you can see that can't be
shown . . .

All you need is love, love,
Love is all you need...

The music is basically neobaroque, but as full of miscellanea as a *basura* joint bought in a Tangier café: trumpets, saxophones, random noises of the Zen-Cage school, and footnotes from "yeah, yeah, yeah" and "Greensleeves." Several further wrinkles and refinements are added in "I Am the Walrus," which is really the more interesting side of their next single, though it is "Hello, Goodbye" that gets all the plays. "Hello" is a palpable hit on account of its neatly posited dialectics: "I don't know why you say goodbye, I say hello." But "Walrus" takes a much bigger and more significant step toward the abolition of determinacy. It finds grist for its mill in retreaded 1947 Hollywood movie chords, choruses inspired by early laughing-gas dentistry, and "Elementry penguin singing Hare Krishna." Amid the inchoate prenatal or postprandial noises of this "Walrus," the universe resounds with the mighty cry of "I am the eggman" and intimations of the great ooohm, muttered through mink teeth. The record also marks their first tentative exploration of forbidden territory: "boy you been a naughty girl, you let your knickers down."

Musically the most interesting component of "Walrus" is an ostinato chant in the style of the Villa-Lobos Chôros No. 10. Considering their penchant for Villa-Lobos, the Beatles might do well to go to Brazil and commune with his spirit in the same chick-a-ding jungle that gave rise to Milhaud's *Création du monde*.

"Walrus" also turns up in the filmic *Mystery Tour* package, where the idea of carelessness is carried beyond iconoclasm and raised to the status of an organizing principle. The title song and "The Fool on the Hill" represent the Beatles' two current brands of hot and cold running expressionism: on the one hand, "They've got everything you need/Satisfaction guaranteed," and on the other, "The Fool on the Hill/Sees the sun going down and the eyes in his head/See the world spinning round."

Elsewhere in the album, particularly in "Your Mother Should Know," the Beatles reaffirm their ties to the great western tradition of J. Brahms and the close-knit family. "Your mother should know" is the motto, repeated and repeated. ("Repeating then is in everyone, everyone is in repeating," said Gertrude Stein, surely the patron saint of beatles.) The polyphonic "Blue Jay Way" offers variations on this same theme of iteration and reiteration: "Please don't be long please don't you be very long/Please don't be long," with the predictable result that this is one of the longest songs they have ever recorded.

The sheer irrelevance of much of this music suggests that possibility of another put-on, but McCartney has made it quite plain that "Elementry

penguin singing Hare Krishna" and "Love is all you need" constitute an authoritative pronunciamento from Beatle headquarters. "I believe that love is the one thing that can supersede everything else," he explains. "Love is a groove . . . Love is the only natural thing . . . God is in everything. . . . It just happens that I've realized all of this through acid, but it could have been through anything. It really doesn't matter how I made it . . . The final result is all that counts."

Already the Beatles have nearly succeeded in bringing the two mainstreams of music, serious and pop, Bach and barrelhouse, flowing back in the same broad channel—something that hasn't happened since the days when they were dancing *bourrées* in the streets. What a relief it is to turn on a radio and hear the blare of poetry instead of drivel: "Lovely Rita meter maid" or "Expert texpert choking smokers don't you think the joker

laughs at you? Ha ha ha!"

When their revolution is complete and the Beatle millennium arrives, the art of music will once more be a continuum instead of a series of soundproof compartments. For a generation bent on enlarging the spectrum of its sensations, the Beatles—like Beethoven before them—have permanently expanded the limits of the world we live in, the world of vibrations. In years to come, when we look back on this epoch we now think of (tentatively) as the McLuhan era, we shall find that their four faces tower above the scene like Gutzon Borglum's presidents carved from Mount Rushmore, and it shall henceforth be known to posterity as The Age of Beatles.

For further evidence of Frederic Grunfeld's expertise on music, see his article in the Summer, 1967 issue of Horizon *tracing the ancestry of today's omnipresent, twanging guitar.*

QUEEN VICTORIA IN 1876, THE YEAR SHE BECAME EMPRESS OF INDIA, SEATED ON AN IVORY THRONE DONATED BY ONE OF HER SUBJECT PRINCES

THE IMPERIALISTS

They had built an empire forty times the size of their own island, and now, in the
jubilee year, they ruled it in the name of the great queen
and the *Pax Britannica*. Behold here the proud champions of a vanished breed

By JAMES MORRIS

When, on June 22, 1897, Queen Victoria of England celebrated her sixtieth year upon the throne, her ministers of state looked around them at the world of the day, contemplated Her Majesty's place in history, and decided to celebrate the event as a festival of Empire.

It was an obvious focus, to symbolize a reign of such unexampled success. Britain might still be the Two Nations that Disraeli had descried; its slums might still be fetid, its back streets still violent, its industrial cities satanic; but it was in a condition of rare exhilaration all the same, for it was gripped by the excitement of power. The British Empire was the greatest agglomeration of possessions the world had ever known—nearly a quarter of the earth's land mass, nearly a quarter of its population. Given a head start by their original industrial revolution and sustained by the remarkable social and political stability of their kingdom, the British had ringed the globe with their wealth, strength, and pedigree. The lost American Colonies had long since been replaced: half of Asia; half of Africa; half of North America; all of Australia; scattered islands, fortresses, and coaling stations in every ocean—all

these were red on the map, and made Britain by any measure the supreme power of the time.

There were sages who understood that this was a kind of historical inflation—too much consequence chasing too little reality. Britain was an overcrowded island with no natural resources, living by its wits. The circumstances that had made it pre-eminent could not last forever, and one day it must inevitably return to normal. For the moment, though, the British were making the most of their climax. The amorphous creed called the New Imperialism, whose meanings were innumerable, had taken the Conservative-Unionists to a slashing electoral victory over their Liberal opponents, and even the Elgars and Kiplings of the decade were dazzled by the imperial colors. The Empire itself, which patriots of classical tastes liked to call the *Pax Britannica*, was growing all the time like a monumental

snowball, one distant acquisition leading inexorably to another as the fleets and armies of the Crown pressed into another economic market, another strategic hinterland, or another field of Christian endeavor. Asked to define his notion of paradise, Alfred Austin, the poet laureate, probably spoke for the people in his reply: to sit in a garden receiving news alternately of British victories by land and by sea.

And yet, although there was inevitably arrogance in the British air, racial bigotry and vulgar jingoism, still this was a good-natured moment of imperial history. Success had not soured this nation, and behind the gasconade gentler national qualities awaited their turn—humor, toleration, and above all fairness. The queen herself, grandest of all old ladies though she was, perfectly expressed these simpler characteristics, and it was a relief that her message on that Diamond Jubilee morning shrilled to no chauvinist trumpets and did not even pander to the national grandiloquence. She was addressing four hundred and ten million subjects occupying thirteen million square miles of British territory, but all she said was this: "From my heart I thank my people. May God bless them."

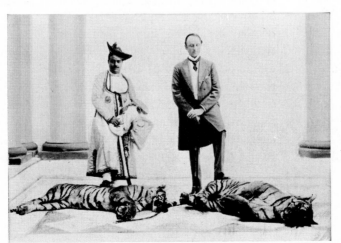

LORD CURZON, VICEROY OF INDIA (1899–1905), AND HUNTING FRIEND

When Kipling first went east from India, he noted that though the stinks of Lahore and Calcutta had something in common, the stink of Burma was different; he was struck by the numberless energies of the Chinese and the startling vigor of Japan, but wherever he went in the eastern Empire, he observed that the British appeared to be exactly the same. "It was just We Our Noble Selves," he wrote sardonically of a party in the barracks above the botanical gardens at Singapore. "In the center was the pretty Memsahib with light hair and fascinating manners, and the plump little Memsahib that talks to everybody and is in everybody's confidence, and the spinster fresh from home, and the bean-fed, well-groomed subaltern with the light coat and the fox-terrier. On the benches sat the fat colonel, and the large judge, and the engineer's wife, and the merchantman and his family after their kind—male and female met I them, and but for the little fact that they were entire strangers to me, I would have saluted them all as old friends." They were just the same people as those he knew in India, except that they were pale from the Singapore climate, "and the veins on the backs of their hands are printed in indigo."

Nobody, of course, runs as true to type as that. The subaltern probably cherished a passion for the poetry of Baudelaire, the spinster may have spoken fluent Cantonese, the merchant and his kind perhaps were Seventh Day Adventists. To the stranger, nevertheless, the British in their Empire do seem to have been instantly familiar, whether they were the stiff, pomaded or parasoled representatives of the gentry or irrepressible soldiers of the line. Britishness was very strong in Victoria's later years, and British people were recognizably British.

For the most part they were bigger and fitter than other Europeans. A prosperous century had made even the poorer classes so, and several hundred years of success had filled out the gentry. The tall stature and upright bearing of the English gentleman are confirmed in every old photograph of regiment, First XV, or Union Committee. Five members of Lord Salisbury's patrician cabinet were more than six feet tall. Salisbury himself was six feet four inches, and Henry Chaplin, his president of the Local Government Board, weighed two hundred and fifty pounds. The average height of army recruits in 1897 was five feet seven inches, and their average chest measurement was thirty-four inches—substantially bigger than the conscripts of the Continental armies. The public-school idea of *mens sana in corpore sano* was percolating, in a desultory way, into the upbringing of the masses, and no other people in Europe were so keen on sport.

These physical advantages were sustained by a detachment of bearing. The most rabid of the new imperialists were quite proud of the fact that the British were not liked: certainly, to be loved was no part of the national ambition. The British were aware that of all the peoples of the earth they were the most commonly resented, but a shell composed of pride, duty, shyness, and a sense of membership protected them. G. W. Steevens, traveling to Egypt in 1897, describes the all-British company on the mail train to Brindisi: "Fair-haired, blue-eyed, spare-shouldered and spare-jawed, with puckered brows and steadfast eyes that seemed to look outwards and inwards at the same time, they were unmistakably builders—British Empire builders." Can one not imagine them, this trainload of bronzed aliens, sharing their private jokes, exuding their particular smells of tweed, tobacco, and lavender, as they presented their baggage to the customs officials at Modane? It is as though they were encapsuled there, snug in their own ways, honoring their own club rules, and rolling securely across Europe to catch their P. and O. Foreigners and subject peoples alike recognized this separateness; it was essential to the character of the *Pax Britannica*. This was not so much a haughty empire as a private one.

The aristocracy of Empire was the official class, together with the landed gentry of British planters, and in crown colonies the two classes often intermarried. It was not a very aristocratic aristocracy. Viceroys and governors were often noblemen, and their wives society beauties—Lady Horton, wife of a governor of Ceylon in the 1830's, was the subject of Byron's "She Walks In Beauty Like the Night." British regiments posted overseas contained their quota of young bloods, but the great mass of the imperial service, like the officer corps of the colonial forces, was pre-eminently upper middle class.

They were the children of a unique culture, that of the English public schools, with its celibate discipline, its classical loyalties, its emphasis on self-reliance, team spirit, delegated responsibility, Christian duty, and stoic control. One did not cry when one said good-bye to Mama at Paddington Station. One did not, as a general rule, wish to appear too clever, or too enthusiastic. One loyally upheld the prefectorial system, while realizing that certain rules were made to be broken. The public schools, greatly expanded in the second half of the century and ever more dedicated to their own code of conduct, lay somewhere near the heart of the imperial ethic. "It would be terrible to think of what would happen to us," wrote Eustace Miles, amateur tennis champion of the world, "if our public school system were swept away, or if —and this comes to very much the same thing—from our public school system were swept away our Athletics and our Games."

A man's best proof of fitness to rule in India, Miles thought, was to have been a captain of games, and certainly the public school system was well suited to the imperial needs. It produced men of high spirits, courage,

AN ENGLISH LADY TAKING A JUMP IN INDIA

and assurance, ready to rough it and unafraid of responsibility. If it was intellectually narrowing and chauvinist, well, this was an empire that survived by the separateness of its rulers, their conviction that what they did was right and that all else was second best. The public-school man was generally able to see the other person's point of view, provided it reflected his own values—*civilized* values, he would say. His inability to grasp the aspirations of Indians, Africans, or Malays stemmed from his absolute certainty that their whole manner of thought or way of life was, through no real fault of their own, misguided. At his worst the public-school man was a snobbish hearty; at his best he combined authority with Christian kindness and what he would have called grit; the rarest of his virtues was human sympathy, the rarest of his vices, cowardice.

And the most irritating of his traits, at least in the imperial context, seems to have been smugness. From the memoirs of the imperial civil services there generally breathes an air of conscious rectitude—disguised often in jollity and boyish dash, but seldom altogether absent. "How is it," one Anglo-Indian asked of himself and his colleagues in a rhetorical question addressed without a blush to his fiancée, who must have loved him dearly, "how is it that these pale-cheeked exiles give security to a race of another hue, other tongues, other religions which rulers of their own people have ever failed to give? Dearest, there are unseen moral causes which I need not point out. . . ."

The imperial protocol was strict and all-embracing (in India sanitary commissioners and inspectors general of jails shared seventy-sixth place in order of precedence), and Baron von Hübner, an Australian traveler of the time, tells us that if ever "members of the lower classes," other than grooms, showed up in Singapore, the government found means of returning them to Britain. White prestige must be maintained, and caste was in the air of Empire.

People of grander imagination often disliked these official airs. Lord Bryce thought the average Indian civil servant pretty boring: "a good deal of uniformity . . . a want of striking, even marked individualities . . . rather wanting in imagination and sympathy . . . too conventionally English." Kitchener infuriated the official ladies of Egypt by preferring the society of glamourous Levantines. Winston Churchill, who was in India in 1896 and 1897, did not take to Anglo-Indian society. "A lot of horrid Anglo-Indian women at the races. Nasty vulgar creatures all looking as though they thought themselves great beauties. I fear me they are a sorry lot. . . . Nice people in India are few and far between. They are like oases in the desert. . . ."

Poor Anglo-Indians! Twenty-one and very clever, Churchill was applying to their provincial attitudes the standards of his own background, glittering with the wealth and genius of London and New York. Life in the official circles of Empire may not have looked exciting to him, but it pursued a staid and comfortable course, much in the tennis-party tradition of the lesser British gentry at home. The scale of things was often grotesquely swollen, though, so that a married couple in India might easily have a staff of twenty-five servants, imposed on them by a caste system even more rigid than their own: bearer, children's nurse, cooks, table servers, a tailor, a laundryman, a water carrier, gardeners, grooms, and grasscutters. In camp, if a fairly senior official took his wife on tour, this establishment might grow to fifty or more dependents. Living in what was virtually a private village with this immense ménage, the imperialist forfeited any kind of privacy—the servants knew everything—and the manner of life remained supremely orthodox. In Ceylon, for example, people were normally "at home" once each week, and there were frequent calls and dances at the Queen's in Kandy and golfing weekends at Nuwara Eliya. The bungalows were lofty and cool and lapped in lawns, and there was an English vicar at the church up the road; all seemed changeless, useful, and very agreeable.

The family tradition was strong in the imperial service. The same names appear repeatedly in the honors lists and church memorials, and fathers' footsteps were loyally followed. The two Napier brothers in the Indian Army were the sons of Lord Napier of Magdala, who had served in the Mutiny and virtually created the hill station of Darjeeling. General Henry Rundle, Kitchener's chief of staff in the Sudan in 1897, was the son of Joseph Rundle, who had first planted the British flag on Aden soil in 1839. Generations of Stracheys had served in India, and there had been a Skinner in the 1st Bengal Lancers ever since Lieutenant Colonel James Skinner founded the regiment as Skinner's Horse in 1803.

This imperial elite was, as conquerors go, very well behaved. Its values were solid. Its rules were mostly sensible. Corruption was rare, and what Churchill thought vulgar was often no more than a dogged determination to stick to the habits and traditions that gave the Empire its stability. There are worse sins for a ruling class than thinking yourself more beautiful than you are.

FACES OF EMPIRE

Let us look at a few faces from the imperial gallery of the nineties, chosen at random from a vestry and a railway camp, a Spy cartoon, an African police station, and a settlement of the Australian outback. Here, for a start, are the archdeacon and the bishop of Madras, as the offices happened to be filled in 1897. The archdeacon was William Weston Elwes, who has a fiery eye, a jutting beard, shoulders powerfully thrust back—the very image of the fighting Christian. The bishop was Frederick Gell, who looks like a highly intelligent dromedary, with a wispy fringe of beard around his chin and an elongated, high-browed, droopy, reproachful face.

Or here is Ronald Preston, the railhead engineer of the Uganda Railway, then encamped with his gangs halfway to Lake Victoria from the sea. We see him sitting at the entrance to his tent with his wife Florence, wearing a linen suit and holding a gun across his knees. He has prominent teeth and large ears, and all around him are trophies of the hunt—zebra skins, antelope horns, and hides. He looks lean, loose-limbed, a little sad, as though he has been condemned to live forever under canvas, building railways and shooting animals; and beside him his wife, in a long skirt, leg-of-mutton sleeves, and a little black boater hat, gazes forlornly out of the picture into the surrounding wilderness.

It is the White Rajah of Sarawak, Sir Charles Anthony Brooke, who returns our stare so urbanely from the Spy cartoon that appeared in *Vanity Fair.* What kingly ease of deportment! What perfection of buttoned frock coat! How exquisitely symmetrical the heavy white mustaches and the curled gray hair above the high forehead! Brooke has prominent white eyebrows, bags beneath the eyes, a wrinkled turtle neck, and a bulky cleft jaw; but above all it is the expression of the face that holds our attention—the expression of a man who makes his own rules, in a sphere of action altogether unique, dealing in subjects—he makes us feel—that we know nothing whatsoever about and would be wise not to make foolish comments on.

Haughty in a very different way is "Bobo" Young, an employee of the British South Africa Company in northeastern Rhodesia, who was previously a private in the Scots Guards and a cook in the Bechuanaland Border Police, and who policed his

FREDERICK GELL, BISHOP OF MADRAS

SIR CHARLES BROOKE, RAJAH OF SARAWAK

"BOBO" YOUNG, RHODESIAN COMMISSIONER

tribes with a ferocious *sang-froid*—he once killed twenty-five natives in a single fight. He is pictured against a prisonlike background of a brick wall, sitting with his arms folded, wearing a high-collared military tunic, and squinting sidelong at the camera. He has a waxed mustache like a drill sergeant's; his eyes are fiercely gleaming; and his mouth is set in a sardonic, slightly contemptuous smile such as might shrivel an African chieftain to insignificance, or in another incarnation wither an importunate customer in the cab queue at the Savoy.

And finally, a great lady of Empire, Daisy Bates. Mrs. Bates first set eyes on Australia in the middle nineties. A young Irishwoman of literary leanings and polished manners, she had married an Australian cattle rancher but was to spend her life in the service of the aborigines, whose fate as a people she assumed to be sealed and whose last generations she wished to comfort. She was a woman of truly Victorian resolution and did nothing by half measures, living for years alone among the tribes, learning their languages, accepting the squalors of their society, and never passing judgment. In our picture we see her setting off by camel buggy for a particularly ghastly journey around the Great Australian Bight. Beside the two camels stands a tall and heavily bearded aborigine, smoking a pipe; on the driver's seat is an aboriginal woman all in black, hung about with baggage, pots and pans, shaggy, matted hair protruding from her bonnet. And immaculate beside her sits Mrs. Daisy Bates. Her face is stern, her neck is stiff, her hands are ladylike upon her lap. She wears a high-collared blouse fastened with a ribbon, a severe black coat and skirt down to her ankles, and a white straw hat with a fly-veil over her face. She seldom, indeed, wore anything else. And if the strength of the White Rajah lay in his facial expression, the power of Daisy Bates was in her posture: high up there on her rickety buggy, with aboriginals for company and camels to tow her, she sits superbly, flamboyantly erect, as if to show that a good British upbringing, together with sensible corsetry, could fortify a woman against hell itself.

Powerful figures all six, full of sap or gristle, who brought to the developing Empire a vigor all too often tamed by red tape and the hope of promotion, in the secretariat buildings up the road.

ST. GEORGE'S CATHEDRAL, MADRAS

WILLIAM ELWES, ARCHDEACON OF MADRAS

FROM *The Iron Snake* BY R. HARDY, COLLINS, LONDON

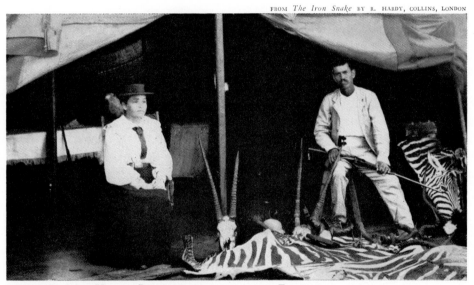

RONALD PRESTON, UGANDA RAILWAY BUILDER, AND WIFE FLORENCE

DAISY BATES AND ABORIGINE COMPANIONS ON AN AUSTRALIAN EXPEDITION BY CAMEL BUGGY

FROM *The Passing of the Aborigines* BY DAISY BATES, JOHN MURRAY LTD.

On Diamond Jubilee day, June 22, 1897, Queen Victoria's procession halts before a throng of Anglican churchmen, including several American bishops, gathered on the steps of St. Paul's cathedral. The immense procession, which included troops from all parts of the Empire, escorted the queen on a state visit to the City of London. In the plain carriage with Victoria sit her daughter-in-law the princess of Wales, and her daughter Helena, the wife of Prince Christian of Schleswig-Holstein. Mounted on glistening steeds, foreground, are many of

Victoria's royal kinsmen, including, at front center, her aging son and heir, the Prince of Wales. Facing the queen, on horseback at right, is Field Marshal Lord Wolseley, commander in chief of the British Army (see pages 70–71); at the far left, on his white Arab charger, Vonolel, is Field Marshal Lord Roberts (see pages 72–73). In the box at right, above the beefeaters, are the foreign ambassadors, including (in morning dress, without ribbons) the U.S. Ambassador, Col. John Hay. The painting is by Andrew Carrick Gow.

67

HENRY MORTON STANLEY WITH HIS GUNBEARER, KALULU

The Explorers: Stanley and Eyre

The age of the great explorers was almost over, but there still lived in England one or two of the giants. Sir Henry Stanley, deliverer of Livingstone, first man to cross Africa from coast to coast, namer of lakes and discoverer of mountains, was an inconspicuous Liberal-Unionist backbencher whose election platform had been "the maintenance, the spread, the dignity, the usefulness of the British Empire." He was fifty-six, a bullet-headed man with a truculent mouth and a walrus mustache, broadly built and very hard of eye. Nobody in England had led a more extraordinary life. Born John Rowlands in Denbighshire, North Wales, he spent nine years of childhood in the St. Asaph workhouse, his father dead and his mother uninterested, under the care of a savage schoolmaster who later went mad. He ran away and worked on a farm, in a haberdasher's shop and a butcher's, and in 1859 sailed as a cabin boy from Liverpool to New Orleans. In America he was adopted by a kind cotton broker and took his name, only to be left on his own again when the elder Stanley died. A life of staggering adventure followed: war, on both sides of the American Civil War, in the Indian campaigns of the West, in the United States Navy; journalism, with Napier in Abyssinia, in Spain during the 1869 rising, in search of Livingstone for the New York *Herald;* African exploration of the most sensational kind; wealth, fame, and the long struggle for recognition and respect in England.

By the late nineties his fighting days were over and he had become an eminent citizen of mild benevolence, reassuming British nationality and marrying very respectably. Though the British Empire had not yet recognized his services with a knighthood, he was loaded with honorary degrees, and Queen Victoria had herself commissioned a portrait of him, to hang in Windsor Castle. We hear nothing of him in the jubilee celebrations, though we may assume he joined his fellow M.P.'s to watch the procession go by. But it is enthralling to think of him there at all, with his memories of workhouse and celebrity; the colossal journeys into the heart of Africa; the meeting with Livingstone that was to become a part of the folklore; the expedition to rescue Emin Pasha, beleaguered by the Mahdi in the Sudan, that cost five thousand lives. Stanley's journey across Africa in the 1870's had led directly to the "scramble for Africa" that was the mainspring of the new imperialism. He was the greatest adventurer of the age, an imperial monument in himself.

*   *   *

Edward Eyre was still alive, too, an imperial specimen of a different sort, whose name had been given to a large bump on the southern Australian shoreline, Eyre Peninsula. Eyre was a Yorkshireman who emigrated to Australia, aged seventeen, with £400. He farmed for a time, served as a magistrate and "protector of aborigines," and discovered a livestock route from New South Wales to the new settlements in South Australia. Then, in 1841, he set off on one of the most desperate of all exploratory journeys, from Adelaide around the Great Australian Bight to King George Sound in the extreme southwest. One white man and three native boys started with him, but presently two of the boys murdered the white overseer and fled with most of the supplies.

Eyre was left with a single aborigine, forty pounds of flour, some tea, and some sugar, with five hundred miles of waterless desert behind him and six hundred ahead. For eight weeks the two men labored across that terrible slab of country. Often they were reduced to gathering the morning dew in a sponge and sucking it. At Thistle Cove they were picked up by a French whaler and rested for ten days on board, but Eyre insisted on finishing the journey and after five months on the march stumbled at last into the settlement at King George Sound. It was a perfectly useless adventure, as it turned out. Nothing was discovered and nothing proved; but Eyre had made his name as one of the most intrepid of the imperial explorers.

By 1897 he was unfortunately best known in England for other reasons. Eyre became lieutenant governor of New Zealand, governor of St. Vincent, and finally governor of Jamaica; and there, in 1865, he put down a Negro riot with unusually ferocious zeal, killing or executing more than six hundred people, flogging six hundred more, and burning down a thousand homes. He became a figure of violent controversy at home. Ruskin, Tennyson, and Carlyle were among his supporters; John Stuart Mill and T. H. Huxley were members of a committee that secured his prosecution for murder. The Eyre Defense Committee called him "a good, humane, and valiant man." The Jamaica Committee, supported by a strong body of what Carlyle called "nigger-philanthropists," hounded him for ten years with accusations of brutality. The legal charges were dismissed, but Eyre was never offered another post. In 1897 he was living in seclusion in a Devonshire manor house, a strange, always dignified, and self-contained man. Through it all he had hardly bothered to defend himself—as though the sandy silence of the outback had muffled his soul.

Edward John Eyre in 1867

GENERAL GARNET JOSEPH WOLSELEY, LATER 1ST VISCOUNT WOLSELEY, IN 1880

THE SOLDIERS: WOLSELEY OF CAIRO

There were only three British soldiers whose personalities had caught the fancy of the public. None had held command in a major war against equal enemies; but they had all distinguished themselves in campaigns against black, brown, or yellow men, and their fame was raised to theatrical height by the new martial pride of the British.

The first was Garnet Wolseley, commander in chief of the British Army, who had been fighting small wars, on and off, for forty-five years. He was Anglo-Irish and loved a good fight—"all other pleasures pale," he once wrote, "before the intense, the maddening delight of leading men into the midst of an enemy, or to the assault of some well-defended place." The first business of any ambitious young officer, he thought, was to try to get himself killed, and this intent he pursued himself, in the Burma War of 1852, the Crimean War, the Indian Mutiny, the China War of 1860, the American Civil War, the Canadian rebellion of 1869, the Ashanti War of 1873, and the Zulu War of 1879. In 1882 his supreme mo-

ment came. Arabi Pasha rose in rebellion against the Egyptian government. The British intervened, and in a brilliant, brief action Wolseley, attacking Arabi from the Suez Canal, defeated him handsomely at Tell el-Kebir, occupied Cairo, and established the British presence in Egypt. He was given a government grant of £30,000, created Baron Wolseley of Cairo and Wolseley, and became a popular hero. It was Wolseley who was celebrated as "The Modern Major General" in Gilbert and Sullivan's *Pirates of Penzance*, and in the slang of the day "all Sir Garnet" meant "all correct." Even his failure to reach Khartoum in time to rescue Gordon in 1884 did not cost him his public popularity, though it made him many enemies in the army.

Wolseley was the late Victorian soldier par excellence. Technically he was a reformer and something of a prophet. Temperamentally he was arrogant, snobbish, insensitive. Intellectually he was not only exceedingly methodical but also deeply religious, with a sense of dedication never quite

fulfilled. He relied on favorites in the army, erecting around himself a "Wolseley ring" of officers who had served with him in old campaigns. Some military critics thought him a fraud, some believed him to be the only great commander of the day who would, in action in a great war, have proved himself a Marlborough or a Wellington. By 1897, at sixty-four, Wolseley was a disillusioned man. He thought his luck had turned with his failure before Khartoum, and he was very conscious of his waning powers. Even his reforming zeal, once so virile and direct, seemed to have lost its bite, and jogging along in the jubilee procession we see his long, melancholy face rather like the White Knight's, sagging a little at the jowls —its mustache, its eyebrows, the shape of its eyes, the hang of its mouth, all drooping sadly with advancing age, beneath the plumed cocked-hat of a field marshal. He was commander in chief of the British Army but not, as he was once said to have imagined himself, Duke of Khartoum.

FROM *Art Journal*, LONDON, 1898

WOLSELEY SURVEYING THE DEFEATED EGYPTIANS AFTER THE BATTLE OF TELL EL-KEBIR, 1882

71

THE SOLDIERS: ROBERTS OF KANDAHAR

The second soldier of the Empire was Field Marshal Lord Roberts of Kandahar, commander in chief in Ireland and the most popular man in the British Army. Where Wolseley was daunting, Roberts was endearing. Where Wolseley pressed for change and efficiency, Roberts stood for the old traditions. Wolseley's professional appeal was to experts or to his own tight circle of intimates; Roberts was above all beloved of his private soldiers, who called him Bobs. Wolseley was tall and overbearing. Roberts was small, simple, sweet-natured. If Gilbert caustically honored Wolseley with "The Modern Major General," Kipling serenaded Roberts with "Bobs":

There's a little red-faced man,
      Which is Bobs,
Rides the tallest 'orse 'e can—
      Our Bobs
If it bucks or kicks or rears,
'E can sit for twenty years
With a smile round both 'is ears—
      Can't yer, Bobs?

Then 'ere's to Bobs Bahadur—little Bobs,

Bobs, Bobs!
'E's our pukka Kandaharder—
      Fightin' Bobs, Bobs, Bobs!

*   *   *

Roberts was another Anglo-Irishman, the son of a general, educated at Eton and Sandhurst and destined to spend his entire life in the imperial service. Until he assumed his Irish command in 1895, he had never served in Europe—such was the range of a British military career in those days. He was old enough to have taken his commission in the East India Company's Bengal Artillery. He served in the Indian Mutiny, in a campaign obscurely remembered as "the Umbeyla campaign against the Sitana Fanatics," in the first Afghan War of 1841, in Napier's Abyssinian expedition, and in 1878 he commanded the army that occupied Afghanistan in the second British attempt to master that intractable power. When, in 1880, the Afghans fell upon the British garrison at Kandahar, Roberts took ten thousand men on an epic relief-march from Kabul.

As Tell el-Kebir was to Wolseley, the march to Kandahar was to Frederick Roberts. It caught the public imagination. Mounted on his white Arab, the very horse we have already seen in the jubilee procession, the trim little image of Bobs rode through the imperial sagas, smiling and imperturbable under the gaunt Afghan hills, with ten thousand faithful tommies at his heels and a horde of brown savages waiting to be routed at the other end. Roberts became commander in chief in India, devoting several years to the problems of imperial defense against the Russians, and after forty-one years of Indian service he came home a hero—devout, happily married, victorious, and teetotal:

'E's a little down on drink,
Chaplain Bobs;
But it keeps us outer Clink—
Don't it, Bobs?
So we will not complain
Tho' 'e's water on the brain
If 'e leads us straight again—
Blue-light Bobs.

MOUNTED ON VONOLEL, ROBERTS LEADS THE MARCH TO RELIEVE KANDAHAR IN THE AFGHAN WAR OF 1880

GENERAL LORD ROBERTS, PORTRAYED BY SARGENT, 1904

AFTER HIS VICTORY AT KHARTOUM, HERBERT KITCHENER (SECOND FROM LEFT) WENT ON TO COMMAND BRITAIN'S FORCES IN INDIA. OF THE AIDES SHOWN WITH HIM

The Soldiers:
Kitchener of Khartoum

Behind the two aging marshals stood the third of the imperial soldiers, and the most formidable: Herbert Kitchener. He was yet another Anglo-Irishman, another soldier's son, but in no other way did he resemble his peers. Set beside Wolseley's languid elegance, or the neat genial precision of Bobs, Kitchener looks a kind of ogre. He was only forty-eight in 1897, but around him a mystique had arisen, a glamour that set him apart from other soldiers and made him one of the figureheads of the new imperialism. He was huge in stature—six feet two inches in his socks—and terrible of visage, and his life was powered by an overriding and ceaseless ambition. He was aloof to women. He did not care whether his colleagues, his subordinates, or his common soldiers loved or loathed him. He had made his early reputation by a series of romantically mysterious adventures among the Arabs—first in Palestine, then in the Sudan—in which he improbably passed himself off as an Arab and undertook various dashing intelligence missions. He had fought under Wolseley in the unsuccessful campaign to relieve Gordon; he had become sirdar of the Egyptian army; he was now, with heavy-footed thoroughness, slowly moving up the Nile, month by month, cataract by cataract, toward the capture of Khartoum.

Kitchener was not, like Wolseley and Roberts, a familiar figure in England. His allure was remote and enigmatic. He fascinated some women by his cold detachment; he maddened many colleagues by his ruthless determination to succeed. He was a great organizer but a plodding and sometimes irresolute general, and seen over the perspective of the years he appears, far more than the two field marshals, to have been emblematic of his times. He was too large for life. He was like a great idea somehow overplayed, so that it has lost its edge. He had never in his life fought against white men, and there was to the ferocity of his eye, the splendor of his famous mustache, his immense bemedaled figure, and his utterly humorless brand of imperialism—there was to Kitchener, though one might hardly dare say it to his face—something faintly absurd.

75

JOHN ARBUTHNOT FISHER, ADMIRAL OF THE FLEET

Alone among the admirals of the imperial navy stood Sir John Fisher, "Jacky," third sea lord and controller, but about to raise his flag in the battleship *Renown* as commander in chief of the North American and West Indies station. Fisher was the most brilliant, the most disliked, the most beloved, and the most extraordinary of the many remarkable officers of the late Victorian navy. He was a raging individualist in a service full of eccentrics. He was also one of the few British naval officers to approach the problems of his profession intellectually, to interest himself in the higher strategy as well as in the new technology, in the social structure of the service and its part in the *Realpolitik* of the times. Fisher was at once a violently enthusiastic reformer and a sentimental traditionalist. His personal saint was Nelson; one of his many slogans was "Think in oceans, sink at sight," and it was he who, asked one evening at dinner by Queen Victoria what all the laughter was about at the other end of the table, replied instantly without a blush: "I was telling Lady Ely, Ma'am, that I had enough flannel round my tummy to go all round this room."

Fisher's life had been inextricably imperial. He was born in Ceylon, where his father, having retired from the Ceylonese police, had a small coffee estate; and his yellowish complexion and mandarin features seemed to give substance to the legend that his mother was a Singhalese princess (she was in fact the granddaughter of a Lord Mayor of London). His godmother was the governor's wife—that Lady Horton whom Byron had apostrophized. His godfather was commander of the garrison. Two of his brothers entered the Ceylon Civil Service, and two more became naval officers. Before he was forty-one Fisher had served in the Mediterranean, the West Indies, and the Channel Squadron, had attacked the Taku forts on the Peiho river in China, and had commanded the battleship *Inflexi-*

ble, the greatest of her day, in the bombardment of Alexandria.

But though the Empire had made him and he was fast becoming one of the most powerful men in the kingdom, he was hardly a new imperialist. His ebullience was tauter than the rather rambling enthusiasms of the greater Britain school. He thought of Britain essentially as a European power, faced always by potential enemies across the Channel, as it had been in Nelson's day. The imperial duties of policing the seas, showing the flag, and overawing petty potentates did not excite him, for he knew that when the *Pax Britannica* was finally challenged, it would survive only by the most modern naval expertise. He wanted to concentrate the navy's scattered strength in three or four massive fleets. He gave the destroyer its name. He was concerned always with gunpowder, speed, new kinds of boiler, with the menace of the submarine and the aircraft. He had blatant favorites and bêtes noires, devoted disciples and unforgiving enemies. He made shameless use of the press. Wherever he went, whatever command he assumed, he turned things topsy-turvy and shook officers out of their comfortable lethargy. When he commanded the cruiser *Northampton*, so his second-in-command complained, "we had 150 runs with Whitehead torpedoes in the last ten days, and the whole Navy only had 200 last year."

Yet in his person this marvelous man, so obsessed with the severe techniques of his profession, represented almost better than anyone the style of the British Empire, its pungent mixture of quirk, arrogance, and good nature. Fisher was a man of tremendous personal charm. He had a passion for dancing: if no women were present, he would dance with a brother officer, whistling his own music. He loved sermons and was often to be seen in garrison churches hunched formidably in the front pew, eye to eye with the quailing preacher. He

gloried in show: the flurry of foam at the stern of the admiral's barge, as it reversed to the gangplank, the splendor of British battleships sliding into Malta at daybreak, the boyish pleasure of things biggest, fastest, newest. "The Royal Navy always travels first class," he liked to say; it was the best navy in the world, serving the best of countries, and Fisher was never ashamed to show it.

And so transparent was this patriotism, so bluff its expression, and so fascinating Fisher's personality, that to foreigners he seldom gave offense. He was an admiral of the Royal Navy, and that was that. Even more, by the expression on his face, the effortlessly peremptory pose of his body, and the irresistible twinkle in his eye, he seemed to exemplify in his person all that the navy meant to the world. The sultan of Morocco, once paying a visit to Fisher's flagship, was asked afterward what had most impressed him and replied without hesitation: "The Admiral's face." To anyone meeting Fisher for the first time, the British Empire must have seemed perfectly impregnable. There he sits in his chair, a thickset man holding his sword hilt, with his cocked hat across his knee, a cluster of medals on his chest, and a belt buckle embossed with the admiralty crest. His face is an indescribable mixture of sneer, defiance, and humorous bravado. His thick-lipped mouth turns down at the corners. His hair is carefully brushed in a cowlick across his forehead. His nostrils appear to be dilated, like a bull's, and the diagonal creases running down from his nose make him look as though he is finding life perpetually distasteful. Yet if you place your hand over the lower half of the face, you will find that the upper half is alive with laughter: there are laugh lines all around the eyes, the big, clear forehead looks sunny and carefree, and there is something about the expression that makes you feel even now, across the gulf of so many years, that if Fisher's aboard, all's well.

Of the proconsuls in the field of Empire that summer, two in particular would long be remembered: Cromer of Egypt, then in his prime; and Lugard of Africa, still awaiting bigger things—the one a Baring of the banking Barings, the other the son of a chaplain on the Madras establishment.

Frederick Lugard was thirty-nine in 1897 and already famous. Born inside Fort St. George in Madras, he had failed the Indian civil service examination and, helped by his Uncle Edward, permanent undersecretary at the War Office, joined the army instead. But he was not cut out for soldiering. A small, wiry, nervous man, he was adventurous in a solitary way, a fine shot and an irrepressible big-game hunter, and the first ten years of his adult life were unsatisfying. He served under Roberts in Afghanistan, but was ill and saw little fighting. He fought with Wolseley in the Sudan and in Burma in the campaign to unseat Thebaw, the last of the Burmese kings. He tried unsuccessfully to join the Italian forces preparing in 1887 to fight the Abyssinians for the possession of Massaua. He was short of money and in poor health when in 1888 he was invited to join a force raised by the African Lakes Company to protect its interests on Lake Nyasa against the raids of Arab and Swahili slave traders.

At a stroke Lugard became a convinced and dedicated imperialist. He never went back to the army. Instead he joined the British East Africa Company and at thirty-two became virtually the father of British Uganda. He defeated the slavers, established a series of stations from the coast to the Nile, ended the wars between Moslems and Christians, made treaties with the local chiefs, and finally persuaded the British government to assume responsibility for the whole country. He became the trouble shooter of British Africa. In Nigeria he forestalled the French in the occupation of a place called Nikki, beating them to it in a lightning march and securing the British position in western Nigeria. In Bechuanaland he made a fearful journey across the Kalahari Desert, seven hundred miles through country devastated everywhere by the rinderpest, to explore a mineral concession.

Through all this derring-do he was evolving a new theory of imperial government, a concept of indirect rule that would enable the natives to maintain their own social and political forms, refined rather than destroyed by the imperial authority. Under his inspiration indirect rule was carried in Nigeria to a pitch of subtlety and complexity never equaled elsewhere. Lugard began as a mercenary of Empire; but he was already acquiring the habits of an apostle, a dedicated champion of imperial trusteeship, of a paternal imperialism that would allow the native peoples to develop—not in their own time but at least according to their own cultures—while ensuring that the resources of their territories were developed for the benefit of the world as a whole. He was a kind and lonely man, bad at sharing responsibility, excellent at shouldering it. He was one of the very few British theorists of Empire to apply his ideas in the field—the very antithesis of the

HIGHLAND TROOPS AT THE SPHINX IN 1882 DURING THE WAR WITH EGYPT

unobtrusive bureaucrat the Indian civil service might have made of him.

* * *

What a world away was Cromer, whose power we have already glimpsed in Cairo and who was now, at fifty-six, in his fourteenth year as proto-Pharaoh! Cromer was born to authority, the son of an M.P., the grandson of an admiral, and a member of one of London's most distinguished banking families—German, probably Jewish, by origin. He was a ruddy-faced man, with short white hair and trimmed mustache, wearing gold-rimmed spectacles and rather nattily dressed. He looked like a surgeon or perhaps a reliable family solicitor, a serious, calm, and balanced man. The wild vagaries of Egyptian life only threw his composure into greater relief. It was Cromer who, without prejudice and without excitement, had been at the receiving end of Gordon's feverish hates and enthusiasms, telegraphed downriver from the palace at Khartoum; Cromer who stood halfway between Gladstone and Lord Wolseley during the tragic campaign of 1884; Cromer to whom the great Kitchener had sent an urgent cable, only a month or two before the jubilee, asking what he ought to do next, when faced with a tricky military situation up the Nile.

Cromer had started life as a soldier himself, serving first in the Ionian Islands in the days when they were a British protectorate, then in Malta and in Jamaica. He went out to India as private secretary to the viceroy, his cousin Lord Northbrook, and spent a few years in Egypt, before the British occupation, as British member of the Caisse de la Dette. Then, in 1883, he followed Wolseley into Cairo and began his life's work —the reformation and reconstruction of Egypt. He was very grand indeed. In India they had called him Overbaring. In Cairo they nicknamed him Le Grand Ours. Wilfrid Blunt, then resident in Cairo, said his reports were written in a "first chapter of Genesis

FROM *Vanity Fair*, DECEMBER, 1895

FREDERICK, BARON LUGARD, BY SPY

style." He moved with an air of ineffable superiority and disapproved, as D. G. Hogarth wrote, of "fantasy, rhapsody and all kinds of unstable exuberance."

It was his fate to live in a country where every kind of exuberant instability was part of the very climate —a country described by Alfred Milner, Cromer's director general of ac-

NATIONAL PORTRAIT GALLERY, LONDON

EVELYN BARING, EARL OF CROMER

counts, as "unalterably, eternally abnormal." The longer he stayed in Egypt, the loftier Cromer became. "The Egyptians," he wrote, "should be permitted to govern themselves after the fashion in which Europeans think they ought to be governed"— and when he spoke of Europeans, he unquestionably thought first of himself. His mandate of power was indeterminate. His use of it was masterly. He was in practice the absolute ruler of Egypt, in whose presence nationalist aspirations repeatedly withered; giving office to any leading nationalist, Cromer thought, would be "only a little less absurd than the nomination of some savage Red Indian chief to be Governor-General of Canada." Cromer knew what was best for the country, and to the intense irritation of many of his contemporaries, generally seemed to be right. Under his command Egypt escaped from bankruptcy and actually produced a surplus. Great irrigation projects were launched. The Aswan Dam was begun. The Egyptian courts were reformed, forced labor was abolished, the railways were rebuilt, the army was disciplined.

It was paradoxical that in Egypt, the most tenuously indirect of British possessions, British imperialism should have come closest to the classic form of the ancient conquerors: a personal despotism, that is, characterized by the imposition of a new order upon a demoralized people and the building of great engineering works. Almost alone Cromer left this mark upon Egypt, like an off-stage Alexander; for from first to last his official rank was that of consul general of Great Britain, and his modest palace was only the British consulate. The Egyptian princess Nazli Fazil was once visiting her cousin the khedive of Egypt when they heard a shout far down the street and the rattle of wheels. The khedive paled. "Listen," he said, "I hear the cry of the runner in front of Baring's carriage. Who knows what he is coming to tell me?"

BROWN BROTHERS

CECIL RHODES IN THE FIELD DURING THE MATABELE REBELLION OF 1896

There was something almost unreal about the scale of Cecil Rhodes. He was nicknamed the Colossus, of course; and of all the new imperialists, he most looked the part. He had a Roman face: big, prominent of eye, rather sneering—just such a face as a police reconstruction might compose if fed the details of one who was both a diamond millionaire and a kind of emperor. There was a shifty look to Rhodes, but it was shiftiness in the grand manner, as if he dealt in millions always—millions of pounds, millions of square miles, millions of people.

Rhodes scarcely figured in the celebration of the jubilee. By the summer of 1897 he was nearly discredited by his sponsorship of the Jameson Raid, carried out by his assistant and protégé, Leander Starr Jameson. In a premature rehearsal of the Boer War, Jameson had led a band of five hundred men on an expedition to seize the government of the Transvaal. This raid failed, and Jameson was sent to jail, but only after he had charmed half of England by observing with

REQUIEM

There were other exceptional imperialists, of course, waxing or waning in Britain then—politicians like Dilke and Rosebery; future proconsuls like Curzon and Alfred Milner; George Goldie, the Rhodes of the Niger basin; and Frank Swettenham, the Raffles of Malaya. Our chosen celebrities, though, may stand as champions for them all, the stars of the imperial show, a strange and gaudy company of performers above whose nodding plumes and ruthless ambitions there sat only the one supreme imperial presence, Victoria RI.

The queen empress was the image and summit of Empire, revealing in herself many of the strains of the British imperium—proud and often overbearing, but with an unexpected

sweetness at the heart; suburban and sometimes vulgar; sentimental; in old age less beautiful than imposing; girlishly beguiled by the mysteries of the Orient, maternally considerate toward the natives, stubbornly determined to hang on to her possessions; seduced by high words, dazzling persons, lofty projects, colors; impatient of things small, meticulous, or self-effacing. A formidable lady indeed, but old, very old, and portly in her long dresses, so that when she sat sculptured on her throne in the public gardens of Aden or Colombo, Kingston or Melbourne, she seemed less a person than some stylized divinity—a goddess inescapable, glimpsed through screens of banyan trees or rising, tremendous, above banana groves; a god-

dess of wealth, age, power, so old that the world could hardly remember itself without her and had already given her name to an era. She *was* the *Pax Britannica*, and geography recognized the fact with towns called Victoria in South Africa, Labuan, Guiana, Grenada, Honduras, Newfoundland, Nigeria, Vancouver Island; with Victoriaville in Quebec, the Victoria Nile in Uganda, the state of Victoria in Australia; with six Lake Victorias and two Cape Victorias; with Victoria Range, Bay, Strait, Valley, Point, Park, Mine, Peak, Beach, Bridge, County, Cove, Downs, Land, Estate, Falls, Fjord, Gap, Harbor, Headland, Island, and Hill—setting such a seal upon the world, in cartography as in command, as no monarch in the his-

candor: "I know perfectly well that as I have not succeeded the natural thing has happened. I also know that if I had succeeded I should have been forgiven." To many new imperialists he and Rhodes were heroes still, and the raid was seen only as an endearing excess of boyish dash. They expressed for many Britons the grand fling of Empire, skullduggery and all.

Rhodes was first of all a moneymaker. A millionaire before he was thirty-five, he took five years to get his pass degree at Oxford, because he spent so much time supervising his diamond interests in Kimberley. The fifth son of an English country parson, he first went to South Africa to help his brother grow cotton in Natal, where the climate was thought to be better for his asthma; it was only in the second half of his life that he conceived a vision of Empire in some ways more naïve, in some ways nobler, and in all ways more spacious than anyone else's. To Rhodes the British Empire was to be one of the revelations of human history, a new heaven and a new earth. In 1877, at twenty-four, he made his first will, leaving his money for the formation of a secret society to extend British rule across the earth; he foresaw the occupation by British settlers of the entire continent of Africa, the Holy Land, the whole of South America, the islands of the Pacific, the Malay Archipelago, the seaboard of China, and Japan. The United States would be recovered, the whole Empire would be consolidated, everybody would be represented in one imperial parliament, and the whole structure would form "so great a Power as hereafter [to] render wars impossible and promote the best interests of humanity."

Rhodes's achievements fell pitifully short of these Olympian prospects. He failed to build his Cape-to-Cairo railway, or even to unite South Africa under the British flag. His one great political creation, Rhodesia, was presently to prove a disastrous anachronism—a white state set impossibly in a black continent. In 1897 he was forty-four and had fallen to the nadir of his affairs. He was seen by more restrained imperialists as a mere shady speculator, extending his unsavory activities from diamond mining to statesmanship and masking all in high talk. His grand idea, though, survived it all. He really thought of the Empire as an instrument of universal peace. Through all the fluctuations of his fortune, he was perfecting his scheme for the Rhodes Scholarships, which would take "the best men for the world's fight" from the English-speaking countries, send them to Oxford to be polished in England's civilization, and distribute them through the Empire to fulfill his dreams. Of all the new imperialists, Rhodes was the most genuinely inspired. William Blane, the South African poet, wrote truly of this misleading man:

Not from a selfish or sordid ambition
Dreamt he of Empires—in continents
  thought:
His the response to that mystic tuition,
From the great throb of the universe
  caught.

---

tory of mankind had ever set before.

The Diamond Jubilee was an immense success. The queen herself was "deeply touched," so she wrote in her diary, and thought the whole festivity "truly marvelous."

So it was, but soon the immense illusion was to fade; the imperialists would retreat to their northern islands again, and Britain would return to size. Two years later the Boer War broke out, and the certainty of Empire was cracked. Two years after that the queen died, and an era ended. Within twenty years the forces of the Crown were engaged with enemies far more real than any legendary Pathans or Zulus, and regiments that had bestrode the world lay mutilated in French mud. Seventy years later only the rump of Empire remained—a few islands, a fortress or two, a legacy of responsibilities.

All the great glory had gone, and the panoplies had been dismantled. The great queen's statues, emplaced with such fanfare, were quietly removed—sometimes, as at Aden last year, in the dead of night. Imperialism had lost its power to move men's hearts, and the British generally had no regrets as they put the dazzle of it out of their minds, packed away the pith helmets and the camp baths, and returned to a smaller world.

The foregoing article will comprise part of Mr. Morris's new book, Pax Britannica, *which will be published this fall by Harcourt, Brace & World.*

QUEEN VICTORIA TAKES HER LEAVE FROM ADEN, 1967

THE WRECK AT
YASSI ADA

For one George, the ship's captain, the voyage thirteen centuries ago
was a disaster. For another, Dr. George F. Bass,
that disaster presented a chance to pioneer a new branch of archaeology

Sometime during the first half of the seventh century a small Byzantine merchant ship, seventy feet long, scudded southward in a stormy sea along the coast of Asia Minor. The cargo, some nine hundred amphorae —jars for carrying wine—banged about in the hold, and in the cabin a set of balance scales rattled. As she approached a bleak, abandoned island now known as Yassi Ada, a wave drove the ship onto a reef. Its bottom stove in, the ship turned toward the island. The captain may have wondered whether he would have time to rescue forty-odd gold and copper coins from the cabin, but presumably a great gurgle from the hold settled the issue for him. He followed the crew over the side. The captain's name was George, for this name and the words "Senior Sea Captain" were later found inscribed in Greek on the steelyard of the balance scale. One hopes he managed to make off with an amphora. George was certainly a man in need of a drink.

The boat sank on an even keel in one hundred and twenty feet of water. When she hit bottom, she heeled over on her port side. She landed on a steep slope, her bow pointing uphill toward the island she never reached. For the next decade or two, teredos, a kind of underwater termite, nibbled away at the exposed parts of the wooden hull until all that was left of it were bits of its timbers

buried under the sand. The indestructible amphorae, like great ceramic eggs, dropped quietly onto the sandy bottom, roughly filling the area where the ship had been. As the teredos devoured the cabin, the scales dropped among the amphorae and the forty-odd coins rained down over them.

Through a pale-blue Mediterranean Sea (opposite), underwater archaeologists bring up baskets of cargo from a Byzantine merchant ship that sank off the coast of Turkey thirteen centuries ago. The thick tube, suspended by a drum-buoy, "vacuums" the site by sucking up silt. Above, a classical archaeologist in a diving suit, George Bass has spent four summers painstakingly excavating the Byzantine wreck. At 36 he is the chief pioneer in systematic excavation under water.

The wreck remained undisturbed until 1961, when it became the first ship to be excavated systematically by a team of archaeologists working under water. Many ancient wrecks have been salvaged by divers. During the 1950's, for example, the pioneer skin diver Jacques-Yves Cousteau retrieved a Roman wreck off Grand Congloué Island near Marseilles. However, archaeologists have always looked askance at the excavations of nonarchaeologists. Salvage is a word they use with scorn. It was only a matter of time until an archaeologist strapped on scuba gear to take on an underwater dig himself.

Dr. George F. Bass, a classical archaeologist at the University of Pennsylvania in Philadelphia, never had any intention of getting wet for archaeology. But in 1959 Peter Throckmorton, a photographer-journalist who had struck up an acquaintance with some sponge divers in Turkey, informed the University Museum of the University of Pennsylvania about the location of two wrecks—the Byzantine freighter at Yassi Ada, and the wreck of an older ship, a Phoenician merchantman two hundred miles to the south, at Cape Gelidonya. The Cape Gelidonya wreck was loaded with copper and bronze ingots.

Dr. Rodney Young, in charge of the Mediterranean section of the museum, suggested to Bass that he learn to dive. Bass, an amiable South Caro-

ARCHAEOLOGY
UNDER WATER

Bass's two-man submarine, Asherah, is checked out by his assistants, at right. Equipped with cameras, it can survey and map large areas quickly. Once a site is found the divers move in. At center, a diver totes an iron rack forming part of a scaffolding that was built over the site in order to obtain co-ordinated photographs of the dig. Below, a diver stands on the scaffolding to photograph the ship's few surviving timbers. At far right, an artist kneels under water to sketch the site on a sheet of frosted plastic.

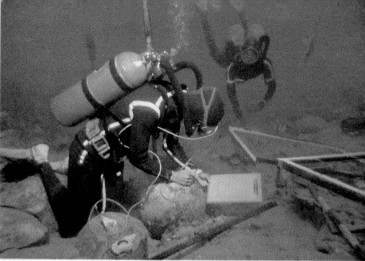

linian who was then in his mid-twenties, had never been below ten feet of water. As with the gentleman who had never been to sea but wound up Admiral of the Queen's Navee, it was fortunate that he persevered in his undertaking. Bass is now the head of the museum's new section of underwater archaeology.

During the summer of 1960 Bass got practical training working with Throckmorton on the excavation of the Phoenician ship off Cape Gelidonya. The excavation resulted in an interesting discovery. The Phoenicians were not thought to have sailed the Mediterranean for several hundred years after the supposed time of the fall of Troy in the twelfth century B.C.; and since Homer referred to Phoenician sailors, many classicists have concluded that Homer wrote about an age well after the Homeric period. But the Phoenician ship, which was dated from 1200 B.C. by pieces of pottery found aboard, indicates that Homer could have written about an age nearer the period of the Trojan War. "Cape Gelidonya proved that underwater archaeology has a real value to scholarship," Bass says.

Bass was the first to apply modern archaeological techniques to underwater excavation. To an extent it is a science of Bass's own making, and he has even written the first textbook on the subject, *Archaeology Under Water*. The early days of underwater archaeology, of which Bass writes with a gently shocked air, were populated with some fairly outlandish events. The first known venture in the field was undertaken in 1446, when Leon Battista Alberti, an architect, tried to run ropes around one of two Roman ships at the bottom of Lake Nemi in Italy. The vessels, one of which was 239 feet long and 78 feet wide, were sumptuously decorated, with mosaics and marble paving over their oak decks and bronze and marble columns in their superstructures. They even had heated baths. Alberti's scheme failed, though he did succeed

in hooking part of a large statue. The boats resisted all attempts at salvage until 1928, when Mussolini, one of the most determined archaeologists on record, had Lake Nemi drained and exposed them to view.

More than half of the known ancient Greek bronzes have come from under water. The bronze "Marathon Boy," which may be by Praxiteles, was hauled up, along with some ancient wreckage, in a fisherman's net in 1925. A wreck off Mahdia, on the coast of North Africa, contained enough Greek art to fill five galleries at the Bardo Museum in Tunis. It also carried a prefabricated Greek temple on its way by sea to some new acropolis. In *Archaeology Under Water* Bass writes with (one feels) restrained enthusiasm, "we wonder what else may still lie beneath the mud."

The mud Bass wonders about most is the mud under the Mediterranean, where there is evidence of sea traffic as far back as 7000 B.C. He estimates that there must be anywhere from ten thousand to one hundred thousand ancient wrecks in the Mediterranean. There are more than a dozen around the Yassi Ada reef alone. Within a few feet of the Byzantine wreck are the remains of another ship a century older. "Between these two wrecks, I found a curious metal bar sticking out of the sand," Bass says. "I thought it was part of my wreck, so I took hold of it. It wouldn't budge, so I dug down. It was still another wreck!"

Up to twenty-five people at a time were involved in the excavation at Yassi Ada. The dig (Bass winces if it is called a swim) took place during the summers from 1961 to 1964. The expedition was subsidized mainly by the University of Pennsylvania Museum and the National Geographic Society.

The base of operations was a black barge anchored one hundred and twenty feet straight up from the wreck on the ocean bottom. The sun-drenched barge with the sandy-col-

ored wooden deck bobbed in the water about a hundred yards offshore. Scuba tanks, fins, and ropes lay about in a busy jumble. Two big Bauer compressors for filling the air tanks or for piping air directly to the divers below hummed constantly.

As a rule, only two divers went down on a shift. Each team could work for only about twenty minutes, twice a day. The water was so clear that Bass could have read a newspaper on the bottom. The wreck was a jumble of amphorae, graceful, long-necked jeroboams of clay; at first sight it looked like a dump littered with oversized Coke bottles. Amphorae, which do not deteriorate like most other cargoes, characterize ancient wrecks. "I got awfully sick of those amphorae," Bass's wife Ann recalls. She spent most of her time cleaning them.

The four-summer dig cost one hundred thousand dollars, which Bass regards as a lot of money for one ship. But as a result of techniques developed at Yassi Ada, he feels that a similar ship could be excavated in a quarter of the time and at a quarter of the cost.

"What removes our work from salvage and makes it archaeology is making detailed plans of the site at every step," Bass says. At first this was done by divers watching over the site and scribbling pictures of amphorae on plastic sheets. The underwater drawing took too much time. The second year Bass turned to underwater photography. But the photographs had to be taken from a constant height if they were to be of any use. Accordingly, Bass built a scaffolding made up of nine rectangular frames placed horizontally above the site; since the wreck was on a slope, the frames looked like a flight of steps. Bass also built a couple of light metal towers, thirteen feet high, with holes at the tops for the camera. The tower bases fitted onto the frames, and the photographic towers could be moved from one step-frame to another, so that pictures could always be taken from the same height and angle (see the diagram at right). Later, stereophotography proved a major breakthrough in mapping.

Working under water has its advantages. For one thing the site is absolutely undisturbed, which is rarely the case on land. Everything in the wreck is likely to be of the same period. And where else can an archaeologist hover over his dig as if he were in a helicopter?

All told, it took slightly more than one thousand hours at the bottom to complete the dig at Yassi Ada—about the same number of hours the dig would have taken on land. Removal of sand, the most time-consuming work, took up almost seven hundred hours. Surprisingly, it is easier to move earth under water than it is on land. Shovels and wheelbarrows are not needed. Instead the divers relied on an air lift, first used on an ancient wreck by Costeau. The air lift works like an underwater vacuum cleaner, sucking up mud and sand from the area of the wreck and spewing it into the water above, where currents carry it away. The air lift was a vertical pipe, forty-five feet high, which rose like a smokestack from a few feet above the center of the wreck; compressed air from the barge raced up the pipe, creating suction. A flexible rubber hose led from the end of the pipe down to the wreck itself. Any archaeologist working with the air hose was surrounded by fish, for it exposed worms in the sand. One of the fish was a big grouper that the divers called the Wreck Fish. It

The sketches of Bass's Yassi Ada site, at right, show how the water helped the archaeologists: the air lift at the center of the top drawing was used as a vacuum cleaner; to its left a lifting balloon effortlessly takes an amphora topside. To even out the undulating slope on which the wreck was strewn, Bass built a step-frame scaffolding (inset) that ensured a precise three-dimensional record of the dig; the fine-screen grids, placed under each photo tower, provided fixed co-ordinates.

CAL SACHS, FROM A DRAWING BY ERIC J. RYAN; INSET, FROM A PAINTING BY PIERRE MION

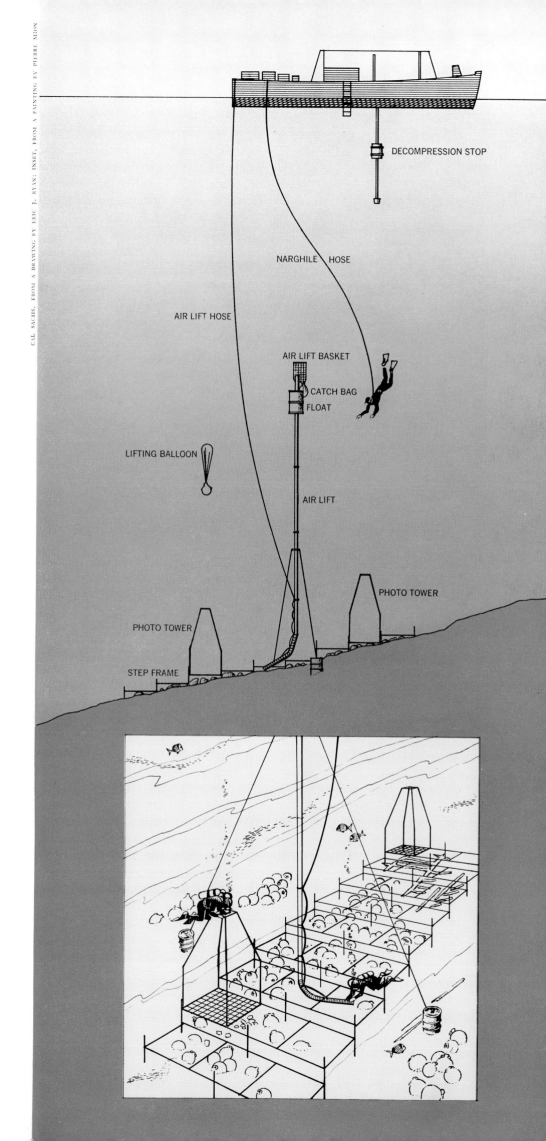

DECOMPRESSION STOP

NARGHILE HOSE

AIR LIFT HOSE

AIR LIFT BASKET

CATCH BAG

FLOAT

LIFTING BALLOON

AIR LIFT

PHOTO TOWER

PHOTO TOWER

STEP FRAME

Ship's yield

Gold coin

Bronze counterweight

Clay wine-sampler

Taking an eye-level survey, Bass (at top) scrutinizes some hard-won fruits of his undersea excavation. The gold coin bears the bust of the emperor Heraclius, ruler of Byzantium from A.D. 610 to 641. The ten-inch statuette, a lead-filled bust of Athena, was used as a counterweight on a set of scales. The wine sampler is a clay pipette, or "wine thief," used for drawing off wine from the amphorae.

hung around for all four summers.

One happy fact of life under water is that objects, when filled with air, bob up to the surface. After an amphora was mapped, the diver would momentarily pop the air hose from his own mouth into the mouth of the amphora and then release it. The amphorae rushed upward with increasing speed until they popped out of the water like fish jumping, to be retrieved by the archaeologists topside. But when a diver was cleaning muck out of an amphora preparatory to its flight, he had to be careful. Moray eels sometimes nestled inside.

Other artifacts were sent above by balloons, each capable of floating four hundred pounds. Like the amphorae, the balloons were inflated at the bottom with compressed air. Balloons brought up the set of balance scales from the ship's cabin and the tiles that had formed the galley roof. Balloons raised concretions, too.

Concretions are in effect casts of rusted iron objects. There were more than one hundred iron objects found in the wreck—including hammers, nails, adzes, and eleven anchors—and almost all of them were rusted away. Before they were completely rusted, however, a concretion of hard-packed shell and sand formed around them, making a mold. These concretions were brought to the surface, cut in half, and filled with a liquid rubber compound that hardened inside. When the concretion was chipped away, a rubber replica of the tool remained.

Other finds, such as the coins or plates and goblets, were simply brought up by the divers themselves. The plates and goblets recovered represent the largest single group of early Byzantine ceramics ever found.

After each dive, the archaeologists were faced with the formidable problem of getting *themselves* up. The most dangerous part of a dive is the ascent. As with any divers, diving archaeologists are apt to get the bends if they rise too quickly. Bass and his men had to stop twice on the way up,

once at a depth of twenty feet for three minutes, and again at ten feet for eighteen minutes. In spite of all precautions at Yassi Ada, the expedition's diving instructor, Larry Joline, got the bends and had to be flown to Istanbul for treatment.

Nonetheless, the divers tended to regard time spent decompressing as time wasted, the same way New Yorkers might view waiting in a stalled subway train. The divers came up with the same solution to their boredom as the subway riders—reading. A pail filled with pocketbooks hung at the ten-foot level. Bass read all of Norman Mailer's *The Deer Park* under water. Paperbacks remained readable under water, the divers found, but afterward they could not be read on land. At the end of one season a diver stayed down an extra half-hour to finish his book.

At very deep wrecks, where decompression stops after individual dives would be prohibitively long, archaeologists will probably live in underwater buildings. Cousteau has had men living in a house 330 feet down, and he hopes soon to have five men dwelling 590 feet down and working in 900 feet of water, with even deeper houses and dives planned for the future. "We already have the know-how," Bass says. "It's just a matter of waiting until a deep wreck comes along that will justify the expense. Perhaps it will be an ancient Greek ship with a load of statues."

Often the sense of excitement and discovery of a dig intensifies when it is over, for an archaeologist does not know exactly what he has found until he gets back to his laboratory. Bass's laboratory is at the University Museum, a big, brown, rambling Romanesque-style building in the heart of Philadelphia. Greek vases, Roman sarcophagi, and Mayan stelae cram the museum from attic to basement. In a basement corridor lined with steampipes and filled with crates a recent visitor pushed open a door

Bass's office was piled high with periodicals and charts. A tall, blonde young woman named Susan Katzev sat on a stool drawing pictures for an article about ancient ships' stoves. Her husband Michael sat at another table, poring over drawings of the tools found in the wreck. He was concentrating on a picture of part of a broken tool. "For all we know, it could be a barnacle scraper, though I have reason to think it's part of either an axe or an adze blade. I wish I knew which." Byzantine axes and adzes are similar; the main difference is that an axe blade fits into its wooden handle vertically, for cutting, while an adze blade fits in sideways, for planing.

"Michael has been trying to figure out whether it's an axe or an adze for a week now," Susan said.

Bass was sitting at his desk going over correspondence pertaining to his next excavation—a Roman wreck, also on the Turkish coast. He said he spent most of his time these days with administration. One of his biggest headaches is fund-raising. In 1964 he raised more than fifty thousand dollars to build a small, two-man submarine, the *Asherah*, for underwater surveying. In its first dives the *Asherah*, which was built by (and partly subsidized by) the Electric Boat Division of General Dynamics, had found nothing more promising than some lobster beds; but Bass was having it fitted out with electronic detection equipment for the summer's expedition and had great hopes for it.

Bass is continually developing new equipment. He pointed to a cardboard dome, about five feet in diameter, that was nestled under a table. This was a model of an invention of his and Michael's—a dome to be placed near the wreck so that the divers could converse under water.

Suddenly Michael gave a shout. "It's an adze," he explained breathlessly. "I've just found a duplicate of my segment attached to its handle, and it's attached sideways, so *both* pieces must be parts of adzes."

Bass smiled. "When something falls into place, you're really excited." Then he frowned slightly. "I get a little bitter," he confided. "I'm doing so much planning for next season that I'm missing out on some of the excitement of the Yassi Ada material. Most of my moments of truth these days have to do with step frames and photo towers."

Bass's visitor wanted to know what the other moments of truth had been. The trickiest assignment had been the job of reconstructing the Byzantine ship on paper. Bass had turned it over to Frederick van Doorninck, chief of operations at Yassi Ada. This was a little like solving a three-dimensional jigsaw puzzle with almost all the pieces missing. But Van Doorninck had been able to get a good idea of the curvature of the bottom of the boat from a close study of wood fragments and nail holes. For the curvature of the sides, he found several angled pieces of ribbing. Then, by projecting the curves of the two sides forward, he computed where the bow would be and how it might have been shaped. There were notches in the ship's bottom that showed where the hatches and cabins above were located. Some tiles at the stern indicated where the cookhouse had been.

When he had done, Van Doorninck had the first accurate picture of a Byzantine ship. It is not a sort seen today. The boat had an asymmetrical hull, fat toward the rear and thin at the forward end, in the Greco-Roman manner. Most important, Van Doorninck was able to show that the boat was transitional between ancient and modern shipbuilding. Modern boats are made by erecting the ribs first and then attaching the hull planks to them. Ancient shipwrights started with the hull planks and then forced the ribs down into them. In the Yassi Ada wreck the bottom was made in the ancient way, but the sides were done the modern way. This, Bass and Van Doorninck believe, shows that the change in shipbuilding was a slow, evolutionary process and not a revolutionary one.

"One matter that's been bothering me is where the boat had come from, where it was going, and what it was doing," Bass said. He was leaning back in his chair with his feet up on the desk. "We have pretty good indication that the boat was coming from Istanbul. We found a pile of empty mussel shells, stacked neatly, among the wreckage. At first we thought they were the remains of local mussels, but then one of our Turkish divers said this type of mussel came only from the water around Istanbul. So it is likely the ship was coming from there. But what's puzzling is, why would a boat coming from Istanbul be carrying a cargo of wine? If anything, wine would be going *to* Istanbul. The amphorae were carrying wine, for we found a pot of resin aboard, and resin was used to line wine amphorae."

Bass's feet hit the floor with a bang. "I've got it!" he said. What had occurred to him was that the boat might have come from Istanbul carrying an Istanbul product, such as grain, in the long-necked amphorae, to trade in the Aegean islands and along the coast of Asia Minor; and that the boat might then have picked up wine to take back to Istanbul.

"That may explain why they had the pot of resin," Bass said exuberantly. "As they sold the grain, they quickly lined the amphorae with resin for the wine they picked up. And it would explain something else, too. I've been wondering why we found only three hundred stoppers for nine hundred amphorae. That means most of the amphorae were empties, or were perhaps carrying grain."

Whatever the answer, the subject was worth pursuing, for one of the main benefits of underwater archaeology is knowledge of ancient trade routes. Bass feels that excavating a boat is every bit as important as excavating a house—more so, perhaps, since what is to be learned about ancient cultures from ships has barely been touched. In *Archaeology Under Water* he writes: "If most of the known monumental Greek bronzes have come from the sea at a time when underwater archaeology is still in its infancy, the promise for the future is clear. Ships have sunk every year since man first floated down a river on a raft, and it is evident that before long a shipwreck of at least every generation of reasonable antiquity will be discovered; later, generations will be reduced to decades. Those ships that contain cargoes datable by coins or other documents will offer the best possible dating for some types of pottery and other artifacts which are so important for dating strata in land excavations. New knowledge of ancient metallurgy, numismatics, metrology, and architecture, as well as sculpture, has resulted already from underwater excavations, and other areas of archaeology will surely profit as well."

Sponge fishermen have turned up almost all of the known ancient wrecks in the Mediterranean. So far, none have been discovered by archaeologists. Bass considers the development of new search techniques the most important problem in underwater archaeology today. Some of the new techniques he has tried are bizarre. Once he towed an underwater television camera behind a boat and spent two months peering into the television screen. "Every moment I expected to see statues," he reported. "All I saw was murk." Then, not content with towing a television camera, Bass had his men towed inside a contraption called a tow vane, a sort of bathysphere with fins on it that skims along the bottom like a trolling plug. Again no luck.

Meanwhile, Professor Harold Edgerton of M.I.T. has had some success with a gadget called a mud pinger, which works something like radar and

can trace a cross section of the sea bottom on a chart. With it, Dr. Edgerton recently discovered an entire classical Greek city, Helice, which sank under the Gulf of Corinth during an earthquake in 373 B.C. Elsewhere in Greece Edgerton has pinged some mud and discovered several blips in the ocean bottom that may well be wreckage. "We're really on to something," Bass said.

There was a squeal of delight from Susan Katzev, who evidently was on to something herself. She had been going over some drawings of odd objects from Yassi Ada. Her husband and Bass peered over her shoulder. "See this hoop-shaped iron fragment?" she said.

Bass and Michael nodded.

She riffled through some pages until she came up with a picture of a rusty, broken padlock. The shackle was missing. "I wonder if the fragment couldn't be the top part of the lock, the part that locks?" she said. "It seems to fit."

Both men agreed that it did.

During the summer of 1967 Bass returned to Yassi Ada with a crew of forty, including the Katzevs, and excavated half the Roman wreck. Conceivably, the new techniques that Bass has developed will allow him to complete the Roman wreck this summer—in half the time it took for the Byzantine wreck. The underwater dome, equipped with a telephone, worked well, and so did a new, high-speed air lift.

Bass described the unfinished dig as frustrating. "We just removed amphorae," he said. "We didn't get to the cookhouse." (In the Byzantine wreck it was near the cookhouse that the tiles, the coins, and the weights were found.) The excavating was frustrating for another reason. Athwart the Roman wreck, Bass found the well-preserved hull of an unidentified ship. Perhaps it is the one at the end of the iron bar he discovered. "All we found aboard was pottery, but whether it's

One of Bass's aides, opposite, scrapes centuries of encrustation off one of the more than nine hundred wine jars that formed the merchantman's chief cargo.

one hundred years old or one thousand years old, I can't say yet."

But the big excitement took place thirteen miles up the coast from Yassi Ada, near Güllük, where sponge divers had found the early Roman statue of the Negro boy in 1962. In previous summers Bass had vainly searched the area with his tow vane in the hope of finding the wreck the statue had come from. Last summer, using a device called a side-scanning sonar, he located the wreck about a mile offshore in three hundred feet of water. Bass is cautious about predicting that there will be more statuary aboard, but he cannot help pointing out that, so far at least, every wreck that has had one work of art in it has had more.

A buoy was dropped to mark the site, and in the *Asherah* two of Bass's staff, Donald Rosencrantz and Yüksel Eğdemir, followed the rope from the buoy down to the ocean floor. In the murky water Rosencrantz made out amphorae and terra-cotta tiles, presumably from the cookhouse. He saw concretions, too, but it was impossible to tell if they contained statuary. However, excavation here may be put off in order to explore other leads that have turned up. With his electronic equipment Bass scanned the area off Marmora where a Hellenistic statue of Demeter had been found, and there were some fifteen promising blips from the ocean bottom.

In the past year, then, underwater archaeology seems to have come of age. Its last major problem—finding sites to excavate—has been overcome. Bass is now admiral of a whole flotilla of promising underwater wrecks.

Henry S. F. Cooper, Jr., has spent a good deal of his time lately around scientists. In the Summer, 1967, HORIZON he wrote about Mt. Palomar. He is a staff writer for The New Yorker.

BOTTICELLI'S
PRIMAVERA

Suppose that a Racine play had survived only as notation for pantomime, or that a Monteverdi opera had come down to us without a title and with only a hint of the libretto. The resulting puzzle would resemble what faces the thousands of tourists who each summer climb the stairs of the Uffizi Gallery in Florence and halt expectantly in front of Sandro Botticelli's *Primavera*. Those who are willing to settle for a poetical tableau and a virtuoso's exercise in arabesques can of course go back to the hotel delighted. But those who want to "read" the mythology are likely to spend the rest of their holidays as art sleuths.

And staying out of the second category of viewers is difficult, for the work is obviously not just painting to dream by. It insists on looking like what it is: an allegory that has been waiting several centuries for the discovery of its original literary inner structure—its precise iconographic program. It needs that program in order to become fully coherent and expressive as visual art, much as an opera score needs a libretto to become musically coherent and expressive.

For whom and when was the picture painted? Does it contain topical allusions? What philosophy guided the artist in his striking mixture of sensuousness and idealism? Who, exactly, are the flower people on the right, the beautiful people on the left, and the young matron in the middle? Is the idealism focused on specific ideals, or is the whole affair merely a vague *quattrocento* love-in? If the return of spring, *la primavera*, is the subject, why are the trees carrying an autumnal load of ripe, golden fruit? There are still no completely satisfactory answers to these and many other questions, and I suppose there never will be, unless a lucky researcher comes across Botticelli's actual "libretto" in a Medicean coffer.

However, this is an excellent time to consider a few of the answers that can be called, for the most part, satisfactory, plus a few that cannot. On the one hand, since World War II brilliant progress toward understanding the painting has been made by professional art historians. On the other hand, this progress has not yet hardened into an orthodox interpretation. It can still be challenged by any sharp-eyed layman who feels that the meaning of a masterpiece is too important to be left entirely to specialists.

Most of the specialists now agree that the *Primavera* was ordered by, or at least for, Lorenzo di Pierfrancesco de' Medici, a second cousin of Lorenzo the Magnificent, and was originally hung in the Medici villa at Castello, on the outskirts of Florence. The Castello property was bought for Lorenzo di Pierfrancesco and his brother in 1477, and that date, or early 1478, seems about right on stylistic grounds for the execution of the picture. The drawing does not have much of the dramatic, wiry vigor that Botticelli favored a couple of years later; it shows instead the tendency toward soft gracefulness that can be seen in the Uffizi's *Adoration of the Magi*, which was probably painted in 1476 or 1477. A comparison of the presumed self-portrait on page 94, which is a detail from the *Adoration*, with the young man's face in the *Primavera* detail on page 102 can make the point.

In fact the only reason for still worrying a little about the commissioning and the date is that Lorenzo di Pierfrancesco was only fifteen years old in 1478. But we know that later in his short life (he died at forty) he patronized both Botticelli and Michelangelo, and we can assume that, being a Medici, he was a precocious connoisseur. Moreover, his age can help to explain the marked didactic tone of the picture. For me at least, there is something in the gesture and look of the central young matron in particular (see detail at right on page 99) that suggests an adult instructing a child.

In 1478, according to the most reliable documents,

By ROY McMULLEN

The artist shows us a dreamy pageant, played by
the flower people of Florence.
But who are they and what are they doing in the woods?

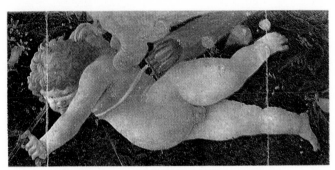

Cupid: A detail from the Primavera

the painter was thirty-three. He had worked with Fra Lippo Lippi and probably Verrocchio, and had apparently had his own workshop since at least 1470. Behind him lay such achievements as the *Fortitude*, the *St. Sebastian*, and the *Adoration* already mentioned. Immediately ahead lay the *St. Augustine*, the frescoes for the Sistine Chapel, the *Mars and Venus*, and *The Birth of Venus*. In other words he was in the midst of one of the most productive periods in his career, and probably the happiest period in his life—although with Botticelli happiness seems to have been relative.

Whatever descriptive label he may have given the *Primavera* has been lost, along with any other external clues about his intentions that he may have provided; and so the usual, and earliest, point of departure for an interpretation is Giorgio Vasari's *Lives*, which were published in 1550, forty years after the death of Botticelli. Vasari says that the painting is about "Venus whom the Graces deck with flowers, denoting spring (*dinotando la primavera*)," which—as a glance at the painting will show—is inaccurate enough to prove that the writer had not been invited out to Castello in quite a while. But the statement is useful because of the mention of Venus, whose presence an ordinary viewer might not suspect. Nearly everybody now agrees that she is the young matron in the middle under the Cupid, although her being fully clothed has provoked a few doubts.

What about "denoting spring"? The phrase certainly accounts for some of the personages and décor, but it leaves enough unexplained to force a conscientious investigator to look into the additional theories that have been proposed. The bulk of these fall into four categories, which can be labeled the Antitheoretical, the Simple, the Topical-Sentimental, and the Intellectual-Astringent.

An extreme example of the Antitheoretical explanation

is the notion that the *Primavera* is merely a botched job —a mixture of motifs without a common denominator. A slightly more plausible and attractive example is the notion that Botticelli, who after all was primarily a painter, ignored a program—concocted perhaps by a Florentine pedant—and unified his work strictly on the basis of shapes, lines, and colors. The weakness, of course, in the "botched" notion is that the picture is not botched, and the weakness in the second notion is that dozens of Botticelli's works show that he was a thinking as well as a painting man.

Vasari's "denoting spring," if that is all he had in mind, might be listed as a Simple theory, but its historical importance really puts it in a category by itself. Anyway, there are other Simple theories. One is that the picture simply celebrates womanhood. Another is that it depicts a meeting of lovers. Still another is that it allegorizes the round of the seasons: you start with the wintry wind on the right, move through spring and summer to autumn, and back through the laden trees to winter again. All of the Simple theories are sweet and poetic, and go well with tapestries and madrigals. All, however, have the defect of being too simple to exhaust the data.

In order to follow any of the Topical-Sentimental theories, which were the favorites of our grandfathers and are still the stock in trade of tourist guides, one must have a system for referring to the cast of characters in the *Primavera*. So, accepting the designations used by the iconologist Edgar Wind, I shall call the puffing god on the right Zephyr; the windblown nymph in his grasp Chloris; the flower woman Flora; the Graces from right to left Pulchritudo, Castitas, and Voluptas; the young man Mercury; and the central figures Venus and Cupid. For this third category of theories one must also keep in mind some Florentine personages, events, and legends that fascinated the imagination of the second half of the

Lorenzo di Pierfrancesco de' Medici, the youthful owner of the Primavera; *from a medal in the Bargello Museum in Florence.*

Botticelli, a presumed self-portrait from the Uffizi Adoration of the Magi, *which he painted several years before the* Primavera.

nineteenth century (especially the English-speaking part of that imagination). The personages are Lorenzo the Magnificent; his handsome, talented, and popular younger brother, Giuliano; the beautiful Simonetta Cattaneo, a Genoese girl who entered Florentine high society as the wife of Marco Vespucci and soon became a favorite of the Medici circle; and the poet Politian, or Poliziano, famous before he was eighteen as the translator of the *Iliad* into Latin.

The first event to remember is the elaborate chivalric tournament, often referred to as The Joust (*La Giostra*) of Giuliano, which the Medici staged in the Piazza Santa Croce in 1475. Giuliano, who won the jousting prize, was dressed in silver armor and equipped with a standard on which Botticelli had depicted Pallas Athena. Simonetta was the tournament Queen of Beauty. Lorenzo's standard bore the motto *Le temps revient* (time returns), and many of the spectators must have felt that their ancient city was entering a marvelous springtime under the guidance of youth: Lorenzo was then twenty-six, and Giuliano and Simonetta were only twenty-two.

Politian, who was just twenty-one, set to work immediately on a long romantic poem, *Stanze per la Giostra di Giuliano de' Medici*, which was destined to become even more famous than the event it celebrated; and one can suppose that the legend that Giuliano and Simonetta were lovers was already in the making. But spring soon proved a treacherous season. The next April La Bella Simonetta died of consumption. April, 1478, brought the murder of Giuliano by enemies of the Medici clan.

Does it not seem reasonable to suppose that these personages and these events are somehow reflected in the *Primavera?* Many people have thought so. The motto *Le temps revient* has been proposed as a probable title for the picture. Mercury, reaching up with his staff to dispel the mists of winter (which are apparently not visible to

all critics), has been identified as Giuliano. Simonetta has been presumed to be Venus, the Queen of Beauty, presiding over the return of spring and hope to Tuscany; or Castitas, the chaste Grace in the middle who is apparently about to be hit by Cupid's flaming arrow and who is perhaps looking longingly at Mercury-Giuliano; or Chloris, in the chill clutch of death or escaping that clutch—in which case the grove becomes a setting in Elysium. The atmosphere and imagery of the picture have been compared with the atmosphere and imagery of Politian's poem, and predictable conclusions drawn. There have even been suggestions that Botticelli himself was half in love with Simonetta. Unfortunately, there is no evidence to support all this lovely speculation.

We are left, then, with the Intellectual-Astringent as the most satisfactory, or the least unsatisfactory, class of theories. Here the major assumptions are that the *Primavera* is primarily a philosophical picture and that the philosophy behind it is Florentine Neo-Platonism. This system of thought mixed a good deal of eclectic mysticism and occultism with such standard Neo-Platonic doctrine as the idea of reaching the heavenly kinds of love and beauty through the earthly kinds. There are documents to support such speculation, but none so far can be called an explicit program for the picture.

One of the most important of these documents was published and analyzed by the art historian E. H. Gombrich in 1945. It is a letter written to Botticelli's patron, the young Lorenzo di Pierfrancesco, by the humanist Marsilio Ficino, apparently sometime in the winter of 1477–78, the period when the *Primavera* was probably painted. Ficino, who at this time had a European reputation as a philosophical translator and commentator, and who had been a mentor of the Medici family since the time of old Cosimo, gives the boy a moral lecture in a wildly pedantic, astrological, and mythological style,

Simonetta, toast of Florence and, some claim, the model for various figures in the Primavera; *portrayed by Piero di Cosimo.*

Marsilio Ficino, whose letter to Lorenzo may have suggested to him the Primavera's *theme; from a painting by Ghirlandaio.*

and closes with a lengthy flourish concerning Venus. She is, he says, not only "a nymph of excellent comeliness," but also the goddess-planet and allegorical figure who stands for Humanity (*Humanitas*) and thus for "Temperance and Honesty, Charm and Splendor."

Gombrich argues persuasively that Botticelli's fully clothed young matron is this Venus-*Humanitas*, a conception perhaps inspired directly by Ficino's letter. The Italian historian Roberto Salvini goes on to conclude that the *Primavera* is "an allegory of the kingdom of Venus, of an ideal world where nature and instinct, embodied by the erotic Zephyr and Flora, are ennobled by culture and civilization, embodied by Venus (Humanity) accompanied by the Graces." He accounts for the presence of Mercury by pointing out that Ficino says the god represents good advice.

This conclusion is hard to quarrel with. But where did Botticelli, or his learned programmers, find the images that convert the abstract philosophy into such a vivid tableau? Gombrich maintains—rather unconvincingly, to my mind—that the source is a passage in Apuleius's *Golden Ass* that describes a pantomime dealing with the Judgment of Paris; and his argument can lead to the conclusion that the picture was meant to be "completed" by the presence in front of it of the real Lorenzo di Pierfrancesco, playing the role of Paris being looked at by Venus. An earlier generation of scholars favored a passage from Lucretius as the source, and of course Politian's verses on the 1475 tournament. More recently, and very convincingly, Wind has argued that "Botticelli's poetical trappings are unmistakably indebted to Politian's muse and to those ancient poems (particularly the Homeric Hymns, Horace's Odes, and Ovid's *Fasti*) with which Politian and Ficino had made him conversant . . ."

If we accept this argument, many of the details and personages—and the philosophical content as well—come

into remarkably sharp focus. On the right Zephyr, as in Ovid, pursues the earth-nymph Chloris. When he touches her, flowers come from her breath, and she is metamorphosed into Flora, the herald of spring. In philosophical terms this triad shows beauty (Flora) emerging from chastity and passion. On the left the dialectic continues with the Graces: Castitas, or chastity, is about to be struck by the blindfolded Cupid's arrow and is being initiated into the mystery of love by Pulchritudo, on her right, and Voluptas, on her left. Meanwhile, still according to Wind, "Venus tempers the dance and keeps its movements within a melodious restraint," for part of the paradox in all this is that the triads of figures on the right and the left are really aspects of the nature of Venus herself.

What about Mercury? Well, one of his roles was leader of the Graces. Also, in the picture he seems to be turning from the world toward the Beyond, and touching the divine clouds through which we humans half glimpse heavenly truths. I admit that Mercury still worries me, and so does the golden fruit. To explain it, as some experts do, as simply the oranges with which Renaissance mythologists identified the golden apples of the Hesperides brings me back to a suspicion I would like to be rid of—namely, the suspicion that the *Primavera* may after all have something to do with the Judgment of Paris. Paris did give one of those apples to Venus.

None of the theories I have mentioned, including the Simonetta speculation, can be called absolutely impossible. As a matter of fact, even if we did have Botticelli's "libretto," we could not be entirely certain of the interpretation that was expounded to the young Lorenzo di Pierfrancesco. Gombrich's research makes it plain that the learned men of Florence were inclined to indulge in extremely freewheeling exegesis; we must therefore imagine Ficino improvising one explanation one day and another the next day, according to the sermon he wished to preach.

Along with the ambiguity in the allegorical meaning, there is an ambiguity in the general emotional tone of the painting. This other ambiguity can be called historical, since the dominant mood seems to vibrate between the Renaissance and the Middle Ages. But it is also a kind of ambiguity peculiar to Florence and to Botticelli.

The *Primavera* certainly qualifies as a Renaissance painting. It exhibits a Renaissance delight in sensuous experience: we can infer that the artist loved flowers with a truly Shakespearean ardor (see the details on pages 100–101 and 104) and that he enjoyed music and the dance—his arabesques, the stylized attitudes of his personages and even their hand gestures (see pages 98–99), have a melodic and balletic quality. That he was interested in the current revival of Greek and Roman culture seems established by the ease with which scholars have found visual allusions to ancient authors, and also perhaps by the hint of a classical frieze in the draperies and in the rhythmic grouping of the figures.

On the other hand, the painting can qualify almost equally well as a medieval production. Venus-*Humanitas* does not look at all pagan; with the leafy arch behind her she looks much like a Madonna in a niche in a medieval church. The three Graces, supplied with wings, would make excellent Gothic angels. Mercury could pass for a Christian saint, although perhaps not as a martyr. Chloris and Zephyr have reminded at least one critic of a desperate soul pursued by a devil. Even if we rule out these recollections of the Christian art of the preceding centuries, other medieval elements can be found. The setting might be one of the allegorical gardens created by the poets celebrating courtly love, and this is a reminder that a fondness for flowers, spring, music, and dancing was by no means confined to the Renaissance. If the composition suggests a classical frieze, it suggests even more a late Gothic tapestry.

And finally, the shallow picture-space is oddly archaic in comparison with the organized deep space of such fifteenth-century avant-gardists as Uccello and Piero della Francesca. Looking at it, we understand a comment by Botticelli's Florentine contemporary Leonardo da Vinci: "Sandro, you tell us not why some things appear lower than others. . . ." Yet we know that Botticelli was capable of obeying the recently invented laws of linear perspective, for some of his paintings are almost academic in their orthodox handling of space.

We must be careful not to overdramatize the pictorial evidence and discover a spiritual conflict in what is merely a pleasant mixture of old and new styles in art. But there is plenty of external evidence that when the *Primavera* was being painted a medieval-Renaissance, or Christian-pagan, conflict was under way in the minds of many devout Florentines. We cannot suppose that the puritanical religious revival led by Savonarola arose from nothing. Was Botticelli, as early as 1478, already sensitive to the coming crisis?

About all we can say is that there are indications that in some mysterious way he was psychologically and spiritually out of tune with the cultural history he was helping to make. There is evidence, too, that his health was poor, that he was neurotic, and that during the last years of his life he was quite desperately sad and eccentric. His painting style veered back and forth between realism and antirealism to such an extent that experts sometimes disagree by ten years about the date of a well-known work. He appears to have earned large sums as a manufacturer of religious pictures, and to have spent the money recklessly. He was alternately melancholy and ecstatic, and according to Vasari, "fond of sophistry . . . and of playing tricks on his pupils and friends."

A possible conclusion to all this is that the strange charm of the *Primavera* comes from an effort to balance historical and personal tendencies that ultimately could not be balanced. Botticelli never tried to paint this kind of picture again.

This article is Roy McMullen's second contribution to a new HORIZON *series, "Anatomy of a Masterpiece." His first, on El Greco's painting* The Burial of Count Orgaz, *appeared in the Autumn, 1967, issue of* HORIZON.

FIGURES IN A LANDSCAPE

Our *Primavera* portfolio opens, on the opposite page, with a reproduction of the full painting. For convenience of discussion the author uses a standard nomenclature shown in the key at right. The photographs on the following pages show details: the arabesque of the intertwining Graces; the serenity of Venus; the whirlpool of arms and flowers in the merging of Chloris and Flora; the curious solitary gesture of Mercury; and the passionate struggle between Chloris and the puffing god Zephyr—the psychological point of departure for the rest of the picture.

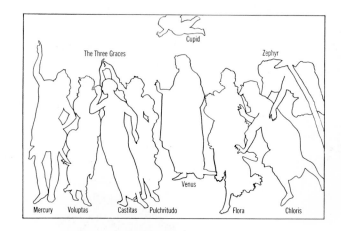

PRIMAVERA

A GRAVURE PORTFOLIO

Botticelli: Primavera, about 1478, on wood panel (6′ 8″ x 10′ 3½″), Uffizi Gallery, Florence

BOTTICELLI: AMATEUR BOTANIST

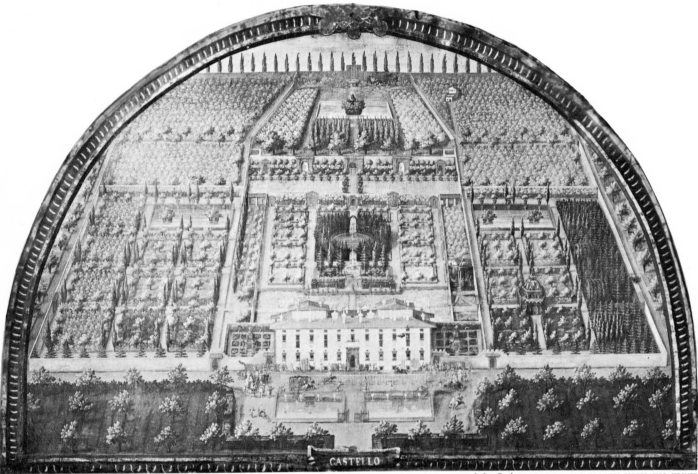

FROM *Italian Gardens* BY GEORGINA MASSON; MUSEO TOPOGRAFICO, FIRENZE

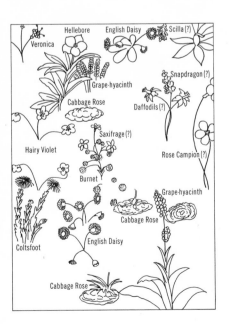

Whatever its meaning as allegory, the *Primavera* clearly expresses a pure sensuous delight in living things—and flowers in particular. Of the forty-odd known species that Botticelli included in the picture several can be identified on the opposite page in a greatly enlarged detail of the ground beneath the left foot of Venus. Their names appear in the key at left. Botticelli may have come to know some of these flowers through discussions with humanists who had studied the works of Dioscorides and other classical botanists; indeed, coltsfoot and hellebore, used as medicines, were known chiefly to scholars and physicians. But he probably discovered many for himself in the gardens and meadows of country villas owned by his chief patrons, the Medici—including the villa of Castello (above), for whose walls the *Primavera* was commissioned. (The painting was hung in one of the rooms overlooking the gardens on the left.)

In the oil lunette above, done in 1599 by the Flemish painter Justus Utens, the gardens appear on a grander scale than they did in Botticelli's day, but the essential features are the same: symmetrical terracing, a central fountain, small "secret gardens" at either end of the house, and thick groves of evergreens for shading. Flowers often grew wild; they were apparently of minor interest to Renaissance gardeners, who were concerned primarily with the neatness of hedges and the ordering of space. It was quite the opposite with Botticelli, who may well have been as expert an amateur botanist as anyone in Florence.

SAVONAROLA:
Reaping the Whirlwind

In permissive societies the revolution often swings the other way, and today's flower children turn into tomorrow's Red Guards. So it happened in Florence in the fifteenth century

Savonarola was memorialized by his follower Fra Bartolommeo in this effigy-portrait, which hangs today in his old cell at San Marco. The inscription beneath reads: "Portrait of Jerome of Ferrara, prophet of God."

By JOSEPH BARRY

Dressed in white robes, carrying olive branches and little scarlet crosses, Savonarola's sacred legion of child inquisitors roamed Renaissance Florence by the regiment, policing the morality of its streets, penetrating its houses. They tore veils and jewelry from women, finery from men. They hounded gamblers, courtesans, and blasphemers and cropped the hair of youths. If a homeowner co-operated, they collected condemned "vanities" peacefully, pronouncing on his house a benediction especially composed by Savonarola. If he did not, they ransacked it for "lascivious" paintings, books, pieces of sculpture, and "pagan" objects. These they threw into the street, mutilating them and piling them in baskets, carting them to the public square for great bonfires that have come to be known as the famous Burning of the Vanities of 1497 and 1498—the greatest catastrophe for Florentine art treasures until the flood that took place in 1966.

Dictator of Florence after the Medici were driven out, Fra Girolamo Savonarola dreamed of making the city the New Jerusalem, of setting the true Christian pattern for the world in opposition to the demoralizing "stench of the sink" of Rome and the Borgia papacy. The Florentines were to become the chosen people with a sacred mission, and Savonarola demanded that they purify themselves as a collective holy example. Such was the mass hysteria—partly due to the eloquence of the Friar—that for almost four years the response was overwhelmingly favorable.

Luca Landucci, a gentle apothecary and devoted follower of the Friar, kept a fascinating diary of the period. "Some boys," he noted on February 7, 1496, "took away a girl's veil-holder in the Via de' Martegli, and her people made a great disturbance about it. This happened because Fra Girolamo had encouraged the boys to oppose the wearing of unsuitable ornaments by women, and to reprove gamblers, so that when anyone said, 'Here come the boys of the *Frate!* every gambler fled, however bold he might be, and the women went about modestly dressed."

Savonarola's teen-age inquisitors with their little red crosses cannot seem too strange a species. The parallel to Mao's Red Guards with their little red bibles springs most readily to mind, but other comparisons might just as easily be made. For part of being adolescent is to be idealistic, and young idealists have always been the ready prey of older moral reformers of both the left and the right.

One still wonders how Florence, heart of that great cultural surge we call the Italian Renaissance, how the cultivated Florentines themselves, "the cleverest people of Italy"—the compliment is Savonarola's—could have come to this. The cowled Dominican monk of the dark complexion; the heavily lashed dark gray eyes, "sometimes giving forth red flashes"; the low, creased forehead; the thick underlip; the gaunt face and great hooked nose of an Aztec warrior; the fleshless, high-strung hands, so emaciated "they looked transparent under the light"—how did this extraordinary figure manage to hold such power?

Girolamo was born in Ferrara in 1452, the precocious child of a household in which the grandfather was a physician, the father a spendthrift. At nineteen he fell in love with the illegitimate daughter of a Strozzi, who disdained marrying a Savonarola. Several years later he stole away to a monastery in Bologna, leaving behind a treatise on "Contempt of the World." Florence first saw Savonarola as a preacher in 1482 and was singularly unimpressed. "Neither his gestures," says Cinozzi, who attended his series of sermons, "nor his speech gave satisfaction." Rough and unadorned, it was far from the Ciceronian style of the Florentine pulpit. "These verbal elegancies and ornaments," said Savonarola stubbornly, "will have to give way to sound doctrines simply preached." When his congregation

dwindled to less than twenty-five, he moved on.

After a long interim in Lombardy and Tuscany, he was recalled by Lorenzo de' Medici to Florence and the monastery of San Marco. By this time fiery prophecy had given him his own effective style, and fame followed. Soon the cloister gardens were too small for his audiences, and he was invited to the pulpit of the great Duomo cathedral. He had found his fulcrum. Rapt in a kind of ecstasy, "an inward fire consuming my bones, compelling me to speak," Savonarola preached of impending disaster, but rapid redemption if Florence and the church were reformed.

The year 1492 was a turning point for the Friar. Two of three deaths he had predicted came about: those of Lorenzo, who had sent for him on his deathbed, and Pope Innocent VIII, a man scarcely better than his Borgia successor. Savonarola had also foretold the death of the king of Naples, which occurred in 1494, a climactic year that brought King Charles of France across the Alps in an invasion of Italy—the new Cyrus also predicted by Savonarola.

The years between the prophecies and their fulfillment consolidated Savonarola's popularity and the sense of the people's dependence on him. As Lorenzo's twenty-two-year-old son Piero, who lacked his father's shrewdness, let the Medici's carefully built political machine fall apart, the Friar became the preacher of the growing party of the opposition. Then Piero made his fatal move. Hurrying to the French camp in person to attempt an eleventh-hour salvation of Florence, he was forced instead to hand over the fortresses of Pisa and Leghorn to the French. Terrified and furious, the Florentines gathered in the streets and squares, some with ancient arms. They flocked to the Duomo, crowding it to the walls. There Savonarola held them and calmed them, and a peaceful revolution was accomplished within the palace of the city's governing body,

the signory, where a single speech by white-haired, commanding Piero Capponi restored the republic. "The moment has come to shake off this baby government," he declared. "Let ambassadors be sent to King Charles. And above all, it must not be forgotten to send Father Savonarola as one of the ambassadors, for he has gained the entire love of the people."

The mission met with middling success. Piero de' Medici rushed back to Florence. He was barred from the signory palace and eventually driven with his cardinal brother, Giovanni, from the city.

The French king entered Florence, a puny figure on a great charger, but at the head of the best army in Europe. He presented his demands to the signory, telling it, "I will sound my trumpets," if they were not met. Whereupon Capponi tore up the proffered treaty in his face, crying, "And we will ring our bells!" calling the people to arms. Finally Savonarola went to the king and awed him by suggesting that he leave before God's anger be aroused; and Charles left.

By now the political aspect of Florence had completely changed. Partisans of the Medici had disappeared as if by magic. The Popular Party ruled over everything, and Savonarola ruled the will of the people. He had prophesied the king's coming and had induced him to depart. These days, says Landucci, his sermons were almost daily, and he had audiences of thirteen to fourteen thousand in the Piazza del Duomo. The population of Florence was about ninety thousand.

With no official post save the pulpit, Savonarola became the lawgiver of Florence, the signory signing the decrees. Taxes were reduced for the lower classes, shops opened for the unemployed, people told to trust in God and so in His prime minister. When he called for a Great Council, one was incorporated in the new republican constitution, which was largely his. The governing councils at this time were composed mostly of the Friar's supporters—called the Piagnoni (snivelers) by the opposing faction of the Arrabbiati.

Triumphant as he was, Savonarola was nonetheless plunged in the deepest depression. The future looked dark. The people and the church were so hardened in sin that the scourge he had prophesied—in a celebrated vision of a flaming sword bending toward a world devastated by famine, bloodshed, and plague—seemed upon them. The real reform had to begin. Not only to save the people of Florence, but the world. (Martin Luther was to appear not long afterward and declare Savonarola a precursor of Protestant doctrine and a martyr of the Reformation.)

"Purify your minds," cried the prior of San Marco as 1494 ended, "and you, the people of Florence, will in this way commence the reform of all Italy, and will spread your wings over the world, bringing reformation to all nations. Remember that the Lord has shown clear signs that He desires a renovation of all things, and that you are the people who have been elected to begin this great work."

His eloquence and the people's fervor were now at the flood. Wasted by fasting and the vigil of nightly visions, Savonarola would fall into a trance at the pulpit, and men and women of every age and class would fall into passionate tears. Again and again the Dominican monk who took notes of the sermons would be forced to close, "I was overcome by weeping and could not go on."

"Florence has become like a monastery," the Mantuan ambassador wrote the Marchese of Mantua. "The Friar has so frightened the people that all have given themselves to devotion. He makes everybody fast three days a week on bread and water, and twice a week on bread and wine. He has made all the young maidens, and many of the married women, betake themselves to convents, so that one sees in Florence only servants and slaves and old crones."

The ambassador of hostile Mantua exaggerated. But such reports were believed by most of Italy, which was also hostile. (Actually, Savonarola called for bread and water on Fridays and no meat on Wednesdays as well, raising so much havoc among the butchers that the state had to lower their taxes.) The enthusiasm for Savonarola in Tuscany was something else. Peasants and nobles for miles around would travel by night to reach Florence for the morning discourse—and find standing room only, outside the vast but crowded Duomo.

The fifty originally wearing the Dominican robes of San Marco were now two hundred and thirty. Many of the new monks came from such families as the Strozzi, the Gondi, the Salviati, the Acciaiuoli, and even the Medici. Others were mature men of literature, art, and science, including Giorgio Vespucci, uncle of the famous navigator.

"What a fire Savonarola must have had," says Jacob Burckhardt, "to lead the Florentines, a people so passionate about culture, to submit to the yoke of such doctrines!" But was it only the fire of his voice that captured intellectuals of the time? Machiavelli, it must be noted, was not among them. But four centuries later G. K. Chesterton, for one, who never heard the voice, was.

"Savonarola," the Catholic essayist and novelist wrote, "is a man whom we shall probably never understand until we know what horror may lie at the heart of civilization . . . [His] thrilling challenge to the luxury of his day went far deeper than the mere question of sin. . . . He saw that the actual crimes were not the only evils: that stolen jewels and poisoned wine and obscene pictures were merely the symptoms; that the disease was the complete dependence upon jewels and wine and pictures . . . [that] the end of it all is the hell of no resistance, the hell of an unfathomable softness . . ."

Moderation was scarcely Savona-

rola's virtue, any more than compromise was one of his principles. He urged the uprooting of gambling, the outlawed but still ruling and ruining passion of the Florentines, by torturing the most obstinate offenders. Servants were to be freed for informing on their masters.

As for that "unmentionable vice," homosexuality, Landucci records that the following law was voted against it: "the first time, the offender to be punished with the *gogna* [exposure on the outer wall of the Bargello prison]; the second time, to be fastened to a pillar, the third time, to be burnt."

In truth, for Savonarola all sexuality was a distraction of the flesh from God; and marriage, despite the dulling effect of habit, offered too many occasions for it. Wives whose husbands refused to let them enter a convent were to refuse themselves to their husbands. And Savonarola publicly fixed periods when all wives were to keep their husbands at a distance: at Advent, Lent, and whenever—which was often—they went to church.

Weddings were no longer occasions for joy. After the ceremony there would be a frugal repast for the few guests permitted, accompanied by a sermon of such effect that, according to Fra Burlamacchi, it was not rare for the young couple to leave the table vowing chastity for a time—and sometimes forever.

Increasingly Savonarola turned toward youth as the fertile field for permanent reform. He began to preach to the young from the pulpit. So many responded that children under ten were advised to stay home, but special rows were reserved for those ten to twenty. Flattered by the Friar's attention, the teen-agers were more quickly and generally won over than the adults. During Lent of 1496, Landucci noted "this wonder: not a boy could be kept in bed in the morning, but all ran to church before their mothers."

With Fra Domenico as his lieutenant, Savonarola organized the youngsters into a sacred legion. Each quarter of Florence had its leader, company, and special banner. In addition, boys were appointed to city-wide posts that gave an odd structure to this inner, infant republic. There were the *pacieri*, or peace officers, charged with maintaining order in church and on the street; the *correttori*, or judges, who handed down sentences and executed them; the *limosinieri*, who collected for the poor; the *lustratori*, who saw to it that crosses and other holy objects in public places were kept clean and properly exposed; and finally the *inquisitori*, whose mission was the major one of imposing spiritual purity on the lives and in the homes of the people.

The young inquisitors proceeded to do what the older magistrates preferred simply to legislate against. They tracked down the gamblers and took away their cards and dice and even their money, which they gave to the poor. They forced their way into the houses, preferably of the rich, and subjected them to their juvenile, inquisitorial taste, as well as to the established list of anathema: cards, dice, mirrors, wigs, carnival masks, perfume, poetry, and so forth.

"If you are doing what is wrong," Savonarola cried from the pulpit, "you have no right to complain. If you are doing right, you have nothing to fear from the children." As for those parents who muttered of sending their sons to someplace like France to remove them from the Friar's influence, he said confidently, "Send them where you will, they will come back!"

But most felt like Landucci. After witnessing an alms-collecting procession of more than six thousand white-robed youths during the carnival of 1496, he added to his diary: "some of my sons were amongst those blessed and pure-minded troops of boys."

Indeed, Savonarola's reform of the children seemed a blessing for the people of Florence, which accounts for their initial approval. Pre-Lent carnival time, particularly under the Medici, had been a wild time of drunkenness and debauchery, when the youth of

Florence took delight in their own special "games."

By day they used to stretch long poles across the streets, refusing to let people pass until they had been given money. Then they would buy food and drink, build bonfires around their poles at night, and feast, dance, and carouse until finally and invariably they ended with the "mad and bestial game" described by the chroniclers—throwing stones at each other in a frenzy, so that no carnival ended without some dead on the ground.

For years the sport had been forbidden, but where past signories had failed, Savonarola succeeded. Shrewdly he substituted religious for carnival activities instead of trying to suppress the games entirely. Where boys had collected for drinks, they now put out poles with bags for alms. Instead of carnival songs, they sang hymns, some of them composed by Savonarola. And for the first time they tested their organization in the giant procession witnessed by Landucci "with so much emotion."

A little saintliness for one's children is not a bad thing. Like Landucci, most parents appreciated it. But a teen-age paragovernmental organization with its own judges, police, and inquisitors was too much—particularly since the Friar had told his young followers that their first obedience was to their Father in heaven, not to their fathers on earth. Thus Savonarola's success became the cause of his eventual failure.

From Rome, on March 26, 1496, Ricciardo Becchi, the Florentine ambassador to the Vatican, solemnly reported to the Council of Ten, which handled foreign affairs: "The pope and the cardinals declare that our city suffers great dishonor and some danger from allowing such license to the Friar, and to the children and to the common people. It is dishonorable to the city that all the world should be able to say that it is governed by a Friar and a troop of children . . ."

The Council of Ten, like the signory

and Great Council, was still composed of Savonarola's partisans, and defended him. Preoccupied with the French king's campaign in any case, the Borgia pope knew enough to bide his time. But even before the ambassador's report had been received, on March 27, a Palm Sunday, Florence saw another procession, which also resulted in failure for Savonarola.

Five thousand boys and a great number of girls, all in white robes, carrying red crosses and olive branches, paraded the streets and crossed the bridges. Landucci reports: "Following them came all the city officials and the heads of the guilds; and after these the rest of the men, and then the women. I do not believe that there was a single man or woman who did not go . . ."

And the biographer Fra Placido Cinozzi added: "So great was the fervor of that day that not children and women alone, but also men of station and position, laying aside all human respect, robed themselves in white garments like the children, and danced and sang before the 'tabernacle' [a painting of Christ on an ass], crying out loud with the children, 'Viva Gesù Cristo, Re nostro!'"

Then, as a climax, all the monks came out of the San Marco convent, where the procession ended as it had begun, "each wearing a garland on his tonsured head," Fra Burlamacchi recorded; "and they formed in a great circle round the entire piazza, dancing and singing psalms."

And all Italy laughed.

More effective than the pope or the college of cardinals at this time was that laughter. For the Florentines, of all Italians, were the most sensitive. They could endure a siege or direct attack but were "too clever," as someone has remarked, "to bear ridicule."

Sensing this, Savonarola bluntly said from his pulpit, "I have made you all become as fools, is it not so? But it is not I who have done this. It is Christ." Defiantly he appealed to the example of David dancing before the ark and declared that "one day I shall make you commit yet greater folly."

That day, though it may not have been what he meant, was the last day of the carnival of 1497.

Exhausted from delivering his famous Advent sermons, Savonarola put Fra Domenico in his place on the Duomo pulpit. From there, in January, 1497, his disciple called on the Florentines to prove their devotion to Christ by making His city the most Christian in the world. This they could do, said Fra Domenico, by cleansing their homes of all the "vanities" still hidden in them. These would be piled in the great piazza of Florence and destroyed the last day before Lent.

For days in advance Savonarola's youth squads made their collections, going from house to house, loading baskets and carts, and hauling them to the square, where they were guarded until the holocaust.

Here in the Piazza della Signoria, Savonarola had an enormous wooden pyramid erected, 60 feet high and 240 feet around. Onto its fifteen levels went the vanities: "luxurious foreign garments, powder from Cyprus and other lascivities" (Burlamacchi); false hair, carnival masks and costumes, lotions and cosmetics, dice, playing cards, "ivory and alabaster chess boards," undergarments, musical instruments, illustrated works of Boccaccio and Petrarch, "works of Latin and vulgar poets," tomes on astrology, witchcraft, and devil worship, portraits and sculptures of Florentine ladies in the nude by some of the great artists of the day.

"An irreplaceable loss for the arts," mourned Vasari fifty years later; "especially painting." And he told how Fra Bartolommeo himself had brought his nude studies to add to the pile, "imitated by Lorenzo di Credi and other Piagnoni artists."

Dmitri Merezhkovski has Botticelli, too, approaching on crutches with a bundle of nude drawings, handing them to Fra Domenico. But it is unconfirmed. What we know is that after he was converted by Savonarola, his canvases became far fewer, his Venus disappearing from them along with her spirit, his mood and style darkening with an acid sorrow that has intrigued critics since Walter Pater with the Botticelli Problem.

Has the number of fine works of art on that famous pyramid of vanities been exaggerated? Possibly. But the collection looked impressive enough—and valuable enough—for a Venetian merchant to offer Savonarola twenty-two thousand florins for it. Indignantly he rejected the offer and had the merchant's own portrait added to the pile.

Then at dawn on February 7, 1497, the great doors of the Duomo swung open, and Savonarola celebrated mass for the assembled thousands. After breakfast, led by hosts of white-clad, hymn-singing children, they joined in a grand procession to the piazza. Here the practiced *pacieri* arranged them in front of the signory palace, putting the smallest children in the highest seats so they could see the spectacle. The *limosinieri* went about "collecting more that day than throughout the year."

At a given signal four guards advanced with flaming torches and applied them to four points of the pyramid. Stuffed with gunpowder, it burst into instant, thundering flames. The signory trumpeters sounded, the palace bells pealed, the multitude shouted, and the carnival of 1497 was over.

Again, at the close of the carnival of 1498, there was a burning of the vanities in the Piazza della Signoria, one of even greater value, according to Burlamacchi, than the previous year's. But this time the procession was harried by the street-roving bullies of the Compagnacci faction, who stripped some boys of their white robes, knocked the red crosses from their hands, struck them with sticks, and pelted them with stones and dead cats.

Scarcely four months after the first Burning, in 1497, the papal bull excommunicating Savonarola had been read in the Duomo. Though declared null and void by the Friar and his followers, it nevertheless had its effect. Even Landucci thought it the better part of discretion not to attend, when Savonarola, after six month's silence, defiantly resumed preaching. And even before the papal bull, a signory hostile to Savonarola had taken office, and his enemies, the Arrabbiati and the Compagnacci factions, defiled his pulpit. On the eve of Ascension Day, 1497, they covered it with dirt, stretched an ass's skin over the cushion, and drove nails upward in the board that he would strike during a sermon.

Savonarola's fall promised to be swifter than his rise, and Florence became wilder than ever in reaction. Taverns filled as churches emptied, tracts and ballads slandered him, and mobs gathered outside his monastery, shouting and throwing stones as the brethren held services. He got some respite in July, 1497, when his supporters were again in power and sought (in vain) to have the pope remove his excommunication.

But meanwhile, famine and plague had come, and in the spring of 1498 another signory was elected that was again hostile to Savonarola.

The final humiliation came in April, 1498. A Franciscan friar, most likely inspired by the Arrabbiati, challenged Savonarola, the Dominican, to prove the truth of his doctrines, which the pope declared heresies, by undergoing the ordeal by fire with him. Savonarola scorned the challenge, but fiercely Fra Domenico took it up. Finally it was Fra Domenico and another Franciscan friar who were to undergo together the ordeal, now ordered by the signory.

The signory, in fact, had cynically concluded that this would be a God-given opportunity for ridding Florence, if not of Savonarola, then of his charismatic influence. During the debate by the council, Antonio Strozzi had seriously offered an alternative "unattended by risk of life." "They might undertake to cross the Arno," he said, "without getting wet." Agnolo de' Bardi remarked that he himself would like to see *all* friars go through the fire. And Giovanni Canacci concluded that the whole thing "makes us the laughing stock of the world."

On April 7, 1498, a great crowd assembled on the Piazza della Signoria for the spectacle. Two huge banks of firewood, twenty-five yards long, had been piled on a raised platform with a narrow passage between them for the two friars. Three hundred soldiers kept the crowd from getting too close. Solemnly the Dominicans, followed by Savonarola, marched in from one side and the Franciscans from the other, "and the people," says Landucci, "awaited the great spectacle."

They awaited and awaited.

"After a wait of several hours," Landucci wrote, "everybody began to wonder. The reason of the delay was some argument between the *Frati*, the Franciscans wishing Fra Domenico to strip himself of all his outer garments, as they declared he was bewitched; this he was ready to do, but then they made another condition, namely, that he should not carry the Host through the fire with him, which showed that they were desirous to avoid the test."

Back and forth they went from the piazza to the palace, seeking a decision as the day waned. Suddenly a storm drenched the piazza. The signory took it as the pretext for declaring that the heavens themselves were against the ordeal, at least at this time. The Franciscans slipped away. But Savonarola tried to lead the same solemn procession back to his monastery.

Cheated of their fireworks, the people were furious. A true prophet, they cried, would have performed a miracle. Savonarola had not; they were finished with him. Had it not been for a few armed followers, he and his fellow monks would not have made it back to the monastery alive.

The next day, decreeing Savonarola's banishment, the Signory sent soldiers for him at the monastery. There a mob had already gathered for an attack. Several disciples begged Savonarola to escape while there was still a chance. He hesitated. In great fear, another cried out that the good shepherd should

Led from the slender stone tower of the Palazzo Vecchio (right) to an improvised scaffold in the piazza outside, Savonarola and two of his disciples were hanged and then burned as heretics in May, 1498. The spectacle was recorded for posterity by an anonymous Florentine painter.

lay down his life to save his flock. Thereupon Savonarola surrendered and was taken to the palace prison.

Interrogated and tortured for eleven days, Savonarola, the signory announced, had confessed to heresy. Landucci's diary tells the rest.

"19th May [1498]. The Pope's envoy and the General of San Marco arrived in Florence, in order to examine Fra Girolamo.

20th May (Sunday). This envoy had him put to the rack, and before he was drawn up he asked him whether the things that he had confessed were true; and the *Frate* replied that they were not, and that he was sent by God. And then they had put him on the rack, and he confessed that he was a sinner, the same as he had said before.

22nd May. It was decided that he should be put to death, and that he should be burnt alive. In the evening a scaffold was made, which covered the whole *ringhiera* of the *Palagio de' Signori* . . .

22nd May (Wednesday morning). . . . The first to be executed was Fra Silvestro, who was hung to the post and one arm of the cross, and there not being much drop, he suffered for some time, repeating "Jesu" many times whilst he was hanging, for the rope did not draw tight nor run well. The second was Fra Domenico of Pescia, who also kept saying "Jesu"; and the third was the *Frate* called a heretic, who did not speak aloud, but to himself, and so he was hung. . . . When all three were hung, Fra Girolamo being in the middle . . . a fire was made on the circular platform round the cross, upon which gunpowder was put and set alight, so that the said fire burst out with a noise of rockets and cracking. In a few hours they were burnt, their legs and arms gradually dropping off; part of their bodies remaining hanging to the chains, a quantity of stones were thrown to make them fall . . ."

The stones were thrown by a mob of singing and dancing boys.

Joseph Barry, an American in Paris, wrote "The Twilight Princess and the Sun King" for the Spring, 1967, HORIZON.

The Assassins' onetime stronghold, the Alamut valley, lies at the foot of the grim, soaring Iranian mountains

TO THE VALLEY OF THE ASSASSINS

Six hundred years after
Marco Polo, two young travelers
find the mountain hideout
of Hasan ibn-al-Sabbah,
whose followers gave their name
to political murder

By TIMOTHY SEVERIN

The mountain trail was narrow, far too narrow for an inexperienced motorcyclist and his justifiably terrified pillion passenger. To make matters worse, a drenching mist had reduced visibility to a few yards and turned the rocky surface of the track into a treacherous slime. On our left the edge of the trail dropped away sharply, and an occasional stone, dislodged by the tires, would clatter and bounce for several seconds before it smashed on the rocks below. Once, through a gap in the mist, we peered down into the abyss and saw the burned-out wreck of a jeep that must have skidded on one of the hairpin turns and tumbled off the trail. Seventy-five miles behind us was Teheran, capital of Iran, and ahead through the mist lay the reason for our venture —the Valley of the Assassins.

My companion—Michael de Larra-

beiti—and I had undertaken a journey to trace Marco Polo's route across Asia, and because the great Venetian traveler had written at length about the legendary valley, Mike and I were determined to visit the place. But the valley was accessible, or so we had been told in Teheran, only by mule train. It had seemed logical that where a mule could go, a motorcycle could go too. Struggling up the mountainside five hours later, we were not so sure.

The valley is a great gash, some twenty-five miles long and from three to ten miles wide, locked in the heart of the Elburz Mountains, which rim the southern end of the Caspian Sea. The spine of the valley is the Alamut river, rising at one end of the gash and cutting its way out at the opposite end of the valley via a spectacular sandstone gorge. This gorge and a half-dozen mule paths are the only routes into the valley and could be defended by a handful of men. For this reason the Alamut valley became in 1090 the headquarters of Hasan ibn-al-Sabbah, better known as the Old Man of the Mountain and First Grand Master of the Assassins.

In the preface to his translation of Omar Khayyám's *Rubáiyát* Edward FitzGerald offers a popular version of Hasan ibn-al-Sabbah's rise to fame. According to this story, Hasan was a fellow student of Omar Khayyám and a certain Nizam-al-Mulk. The three young men made a pact that whoever made his fortune first would share it with the other two. In due course it came about that Nizam-al-Mulk rose to be vizier to the sultan Alp Arslan and became second in power to the sultan. Then Omar Khayyám visited his former schoolmate and reminded him of their agreement. But Khayyám did not ask for riches or political advancement, only that he be allowed to live in the shadow of the vizier's fortune so that he could devote his life to the study of science and the arts. This boon was granted. But when Hasan ibn-al-Sabbah in his turn came to see the vizier, he demanded nothing less than a post in the cabinet. When this was given to him, Hasan used his position to undermine the authority of his benefactor. The final clash came when Hasan, eager to prove his superior ability, promised the sultan that he would prepare the royal budget more quickly and efficiently than Nizam-al-Mulk. Indeed, Hasan would have succeeded had not the vizier at the last moment jumbled together the sheets of Hasan's final ledger. Thus, when he read out his accounts to the sultan, Hasan lost his place, was thrown into confusion, and disgraced.

This story, like most contemporary tales about the Assassins, suffers from the fact that it was the theme of Hasan's enemies. On the other hand the official Assassin version of Hasan's life raises the First Grand Master to semi-divine status. Whatever the case

Hasan ibn-al-Sabbah

may be, Hasan's early career was certainly more prosaic than the storytellers would have us believe, though it is not easy to unravel the twists and turns in his climb to power.

The first important step was taken when Hasan, who is thought to have come from a middle-class background, became a convert to the religious sect known as the Ismailians. A branch of the Shiite Moslems, the Ismailians claimed that Ismail, son of the Imam Jafar, was wrongfully deprived of his inheritance and was therefore the true Seventh Imam, tracing his descent back to the Prophet himself. The religious tenets of the Ismailians were extremely strict, and their spiritual leaders had absolute authority. Hasan rose swiftly in the Ismailian hierarchy, and in 1078 he went to Cairo, where the ruling Fatimid caliphs were themselves Ismailian supporters. At this point the Fatimid caliphate, once the foremost power of Islam, was in decline, weakened by the ineptitude of its leaders and torn by a dispute for succession. Cairo was seething with plots and counterplots, and Hasan took advantage of the turmoil to build up a personal following of dissidents who were attracted to the astute and ambitious visitor. Two years later he suddenly reappeared in Persia, this time at the head of a band of retainers who followed their master on a strange and erratic tour of the country.

Hasan visited isolated Ismailian communities and, significantly, inspected several mountain fortresses. Then, in 1090, he seems to have found what he was looking for in the Alamut valley; there, perched on the side of the valley, was a Seljuk castle that would be impregnable if garrisoned with loyal troops and strengthened with additional fortifications. By now Hasan's odd wanderings had aroused the suspicions of the vizier, the same Nizam-al-Mulk of FitzGerald's tale. An order for Hasan's arrest was sent out, but it came too late. The garrison of the Alamut had defected, and Hasan ibn-al-Sabbah was safely ensconced inside the stronghold. The reign of the Assassins in the Alamut had begun. During the next thirty-four years, it is said, Hasan emerged only twice from his lair.

Two years later the Seljuk sultan Malik Shah (Alp Arslan's son) died, and his vast empire disintegrated into quarreling pieces. From his refuge in the Alamut, Hasan preached adherence to the strict beliefs of Ismailianism and encouraged local Ismailian cells to rise up against their rulers. When the other Ismailian leaders disapproved, he broke away from them and proclaimed that he represented the true belief. To give his independent movement a sense of legitimacy Hasan took up the cause of Prince Nizar, one of the claimants to the Fatimid caliphate. When Prince Nizar was defeated and killed, Hasan promptly announced that the prince's infant son had been smuggled to the Alamut, whence he would one day come forth to lead his people to victory. In the meantime Hasan himself was to be the Grand Master, guardian and spiritual leader of the rebels.

The extraordinary aura of myth, rumor, and religious fanaticism that surrounded Hasan ibn-al-Sabbah in his own lifetime distinguishes him from the run-of-the-mill mountain brigand. With real political skill and an uncanny sense of psychological legerdemain Hasan developed the Nizari Ismailians from an obscure religious minority group into a widely respected brotherhood of believers, responsible only to the Grand Master. He radiated personal magnetism, and he was shrewd enough to discern how he could twist the religious nature of Ismailianism to suit his own purposes. It is quite possible that Hasan himself was a sincere believer in his own creed, but his success lay in the fact that he diverted the Nizaris' intense religious loyalty into absolute obedience to himself. With this cult of personality Hasan ibn-al-Sabbah was the genius of the Assassins, and without him the word "assassin" would never have entered the languages of the West.

The root form of "assassin" is the Arabic word *hashshāshīn*, meaning "those addicted to hashish." By association with Hasan's fanatical followers it came to mean "a person who murders, particularly one who kills an important public figure from fanaticism or for money or other reward," because political murders soon became the hallmark of the Nizari Ismailians. There are several theories about how this association came about: the medieval Crusaders thought that the men whom Hasan sent out to kill his enemies committed their murders under the influence of hashish; contemporary Arab sources give the impression that the Nizari killers were called *hashshāshīn* not because they actually used the drug but because their religious mania resembled nothing so much as the effects of smoking hashish.

Marco Polo's version (see page 115), which received wide currency in the Christian West, describes how the Old Man of the Mountain would have young men drugged and carried into a lush garden filled with dancing girls and flowing with wine, milk, and honey. When the youths awoke they would think themselves in Paradise and thereafter, though returned to their native villages, would obey the Old Man's every command, hoping to return to the garden.

Marco Polo's tale cannot be dismissed as a complete fabrication, since the idea of a secret paradise flowing with milk and honey has obvious affinities with the existence of the green and fertile Alamut valley hidden in the midst of the barren mountains. But though the Alamut valley provided the grain of truth around which the legend was built, the skill of the tale was its appeal to the universal fascination for the concept of an earthly paradise where all sensuous pleasures abound. The wine, milk, and honey, the voluptuous damsels, and, in some versions, the nightingales specially imported to fill the valley with the sweetness of their singing—these were magical ingredients to the medieval imagination, whether Moslem or Christian. As Marco Polo said: "Mohamet assured the Saracens that those who go to Paradise will have beautiful women to their hearts' content to do their bidding and will find there rivers of wine and milk and honey and water."

In Christian Europe, too, there was the long-standing tradition of an Oriental paradise, a luscious garden filled with every delight, from which the angel had driven Adam and Eve. The story of Hasan's secret garden thrilled medieval society. The tale had just the right mixture of horror, fantasy, and exquisite enjoyment, and there was dreadful pleasure in contemplating the idea that the wicked Old Man of the Mountain had warped Paradise to his own evil purposes. Furthermore, the legend provided an explanation for the amazing devotion the Grand Master was able to instill in his followers.

Impressive examples of this devotion were common knowledge during the Middle Ages. Henry, Count of Champagne, was believed to have been invited to visit an Assassin fortress in Syria (the Nizaris spread there during the last years of the eleventh century), and as his host led him around the ramparts, the two leaders discussed the importance of personal devotion from their retainers. To illustrate that he could command instant and absolute obedience, the Assassin sheik turned toward a group of his *fida'i*, or fanat-

ical followers, who were standing on a nearby tower, and with a wave of his arm directed that they should leap from the walls. Without a moment's hesitation the entire group of men jumped straight to their deaths.

This tale may or may not be true, but it was certainly believed by many people, and this was precisely the aim of Assassin policy: to build up a horrendous reputation for themselves. Hasan ibn-al-Sabbah and the Grand Masters who followed him relied not only on the devotion of their *fida'i* but also on a war of nerves, a medieval application of psychological warfare. To compensate for their own numerical inferiority the Assassins seldom allowed themselves to be drawn into open battle. Instead they withdrew into their mountain strongholds until any besieging armies lost heart and went home. This was the defensive side of their strategy. To conduct an offensive the Grand Master would send out hand-picked bands of Nizaris, disguised and carrying concealed weapons, to penetrate the court of a hostile ruler and murder him. The most important aspect of the assassinations was that they were conducted *in public*, as when the Prince of Homs and the Prince of Mosul were both struck down in full view of their subjects in their own mosques. In Nizari policy, assassination, like justice, had not only to be done but had to be seen to be done. Thus other rulers would learn their lesson and not interfere with the plans of the Grand Master.

Among the early victims of Assassin daggers was the man reputed to have been Hasan's schoolmate, the vizier Nizam-al-Mulk. His death was a typical Nizari murder. The vizier was killed at a public audience after an unidentified assailant had approached him as if to present a petition. When the vizier leaned forward to receive the petition, the killer snatched out a dagger and mortally wounded him. In later years Assassins were blamed for the deaths of at least two caliphs, the governors of Aleppo, Baghdad, and

MARCO POLO'S REPORT
OF THE GARDEN OF DELIGHTS

Hasan's earthly paradise, as seen by a fifteenth-century European

He (the Old Man of the Mountains) caused to be made in a valley between two mountains the biggest and most beautiful garden that was ever seen, ornamented with gold and with likenesses of all that is beautiful on earth, and also four conduits, one flowing with wine, one with milk, one with honey, and one with water. Fair ladies were there and damsels, the loveliest in the world, unsurpassed at playing every sort of instrument and at singing and dancing. And he gave his men to understand that this garden was Paradise. That is why he made it after this pattern, because Mahomet assured the Saracens that those who go to Paradise will have beautiful women to their hearts' content to do their bidding and will find there rivers of wine and milk and honey and water. So he ordered this garden made like the Paradise that Mahomet promised to the Saracens, and the Saracens of this country believed that it really was Paradise. No one ever entered this garden except those whom he wished to make Assassins. At the entrance stood a castle so strong that it need not fear any man in the world, and there was no way in except through this castle. The Sheik kept with him at his court all the youths of the country from twelve years old to twenty, all, that is, who shaped well as men at arms. These youths knew well by hearsay that Mahomet their prophet had declared Paradise to be made in such a fashion as I have described, and so they accepted it as truth. Now mark what follows. He used to put some of these youths in this Paradise, four at a time, or ten, or twenty, according as he wished. And this is how he did it. He would give them draughts that sent them to sleep immediately. Then he had them taken and put into the garden, where they were wakened. When they awoke and found themselves in there and saw all the things I told you of, they believed that they really were in Paradise. And the ladies and the damsels stayed with them all the time, singing and making music for their delight and ministering to all their desires. So these youths had all that they wished for and asked nothing better than to remain there.

Now the Sheik held his court with great splendor and magnificence and bore himself most nobly and convinced the simple mountain folk that were around him that he was a prophet; and they believed it to be the truth. And when he wanted emissaries to send on some mission of murder, he would administer the drug to as many as he pleased; and while they slept he had them carried into his palace. When these youths awoke and found themselves within the castle, they were amazed and were by no means glad, for the Paradise from which they had come was not a place that they would ever willingly have left. They went forthwith to the Sheik and humbled themselves before him, as men who believed that he was a great prophet. When he asked them whence they came, they would answer that they had come from Paradise, and that this was in truth the Paradise of which Mahomet had told their ancestors; and they would tell their listeners all that they had found there. And others who heard this and had not been there were filled with a great longing to go to this Paradise; they longed for death so that they might go there . . .

When the Sheik desired the death of some great Lord, he would first try an experiment to find out which of his Assassins was the best. He would send some of them off on a mission in the neighborhood at no great distance with orders to kill such and such a man. They went without demur and did the bidding of their Lord. Then, when they had killed the man, they returned to court—those of them that escaped, for some were caught and put to death. When they had returned to their Lord and had told him that they had faithfully performed their task, the Sheik would make a great feast in their honor. And he knew very well which of them had displayed the greatest zeal, because after each he had sent other of his men as spies to report which was the most daring and the best hand at murdering. Then, in order to bring about the death of the Lord or other man which he desired, he would take some of these Assassins of his and send them wherever he might wish, telling them that he was minded to dispatch them to Paradise; they would go accordingly and kill such and such a man; if they died on their mission, they would go there all the sooner. Those who received such a command obeyed it with a right good will, more readily than anything else they might have been called on to do. . . . Thus it happened that no one ever escaped when the Sheik of the Mountain desired his death.

Khurasan, the son of Nizam-al-Mulk, and sundry emirs, sheiks, muftis, and rich merchants. Their near misses were also impressive. On June 16, 1272, Prince Edward of England, while on Crusade at Acre, was badly wounded with a poisoned dagger; and among the Saracens (who, as more orthodox Moslems, were repugnant to the Nizari Ismailians) the famous Saladin was rescued by his bodyguards from a suicide squad of Assassins who had penetrated to within a few yards of his tent. Louis IX of France, the Holy Roman Emperor Frederick II—the list of near victims goes on and on; and almost every sudden death, whether by illness, knife, poison, or garrote, seems to have been attributed to the malicious intervention of the Assassins. Such accusations are undoubtedly exaggerated, for the turbulent situation of the Middle East encouraged bitter enmities among squabbling princes as well as the wider conflict between Cross and Crescent. Individual rulers, even when officially allied with one another, were not at all averse to sending out their own men to murder their rivals and, when the job was done, blaming the Assassins for the killing. There was seldom any way of tracing the identity of the murderers because few of them ever escaped with their lives. Angry mobs or palace guards cut them down before any questions could be asked.

Toward the end of their reign of terror, which lasted more than one hundred and fifty years, the Nizari Ismailians were accused of selling their services to the highest bidder. Originally, under Hasan ibn-al-Sabbah, the Assassins murdered only to further Nizari policies, but from there it was only a short step to committing murders on behalf of their allies. Naturally, once murder for hire became possible, assassination became a less effective political weapon. There is the story of the potentate who offered the men who came to kill him twice their blood money if they would murder the man who sent them. This was far removed from the ideas of Hasan ibn-al-

Sabbah, who believed that the death of a hostile ruler was a neater way of protecting the Nizari Ismailians than sending an army into the field for a bloody clash in which many men would die. Often, in fact, the actual assassination was not necessary; a threat—the dagger found plunged into the ground beside a sleeping prince, or the ostentatious gift of a winding sheet and a pair of knives—would be enough to make the opposition see reason. Hasan was aware that a co-operative ruler was more useful than a dead one.

When Marco Polo wrote about the sinister Old Man of the Mountain, the power of the Nizari Ismailians had been crushed forty years earlier. Marco Polo was particularly interested in the Assassins because his route to China took him close to the Alamut. The narrow mule track that Mike and I were finding so difficult to negotiate turned off the medieval caravan road and threaded its way up into the mountains, which stretched away in rank upon rank to the north. We expected to find the Alamut valley on the far side of every ridge, but it was not until the afternoon that our path at last began to descend. Then, quite suddenly, we emerged from the mist into brilliant sunshine. There, dropping away beneath our feet, lay a deep valley cleft and the silver thread of a river wriggling between the feet of the mountains. On the other side of the river rose the almost vertical wall of a great razor-topped ridge. This final barrier stood like a gigantic castle battlement, a huge reef of rock running directly across our path, and over the ridge we looked down onto a sea of white clouds pooled between the mountains' crests. The clouds hung like a canopy over what we knew must be another valley, the secret valley of the Assassins. By some trick of the light the flank of the final barrier ridge was glowing with reds, greens, grays, and browns of every shade where the different rock-bands had weathered into a random mixture of colors.

Cautiously we rode down the trail until it reached the riverbank and turned downstream. Our road petered out when the river disappeared between tall cliffs, and there, at the end of the track, we found a tumble-down caravansary and a party of Iranians having a picnic in the shade of a large tree. They invited us to join them and, after a meal of unleavened bread and creamy yoghurt, told us how to find our way into the Valley of the Assassins. First we had to leave our motorcycle behind and wade across the river to a tributary gorge on the far side. After passing through this gorge we would find ourselves on the floor of the Alamut valley. Then, about ten miles up the valley on the left-hand side, they said we would find the "Eagle's Nest," Hasan ibn-al-Sabbah's castle.

It was not too difficult to ford the river, because a line of submerged bolders marked the crossing. But on the other side our difficulties really began. There, sure enough, was the entrance to a narrow, winding gorge that opened like a slender knife thrust in the side of the ridge of many colors. The Alamut river had carved out that gorge—a thousand feet deep and about a quarter of a mile long—and now the river was pouring through like a millrace. Mike and I had no choice but to plunge into the swirling water and thrash our way upstream, holding our cameras above our heads. Once I watched Mike being picked up by the current and tossed about in a graceful pirouette before being deposited with a bump into the shoals. Once we stopped to take some photographs, and Mike suggested that I pose in midstream. The photograph was not a success, for the shutter clicked just as I stepped into a large pothole and disappeared from view.

On the other side of the gorge Mike and I emerged onto a flat, fertile valley floor that gurgled and trickled with rivulets and irrigation channels. It was indeed a green paradise when compared with the harsh mountain slopes, though the lush vegetation made mis-

erable terrain for walking. We blundered about for a couple of hours, falling into muddy ditches and squelching across paddy fields before we chanced to come across a rather surly muleteer who agreed to take us up the valley on his animals.

We spent that night at a small village some five or six miles from the gorge. It was not an experience that I would care to repeat; all night we tossed and turned under the searing fire of bites. Whoever concocted the story about the specially imported nightingales forgot to mention the ravenous insect population of the valley. Our blankets had just been taken from the mules and they crawled with vermin. For reinforcements every crack in the mud floor yielded up its scuttling column of bugs.

The next morning our muleteer suddenly and quite irrationally asked to be paid off, demanding far more money than we had brought with us. He stormed and ranted, and there was little use in haggling or offering to send him the extra cash when we got back to Teheran. The mule driver was determined to make trouble and refused to believe us, even trying to search us for hidden coins. Finally he grabbed Mike's camera and tried to make off with it. This was a mistake. Without a word, Mike and I sprang at him in calculated, flea-bitten fury. The ensuing brawl was very brief, for our opponent had obviously not expected that two Europeans would indulge in what Mike lovingly described as a "punch-up." A few wild blows and the whole affair was over. The muleteer lay on the ground and Mike had his camera back.

The court of enquiry that the village headman convened to investigate the fracas was a solemn affair. The council of elders sat in judgment, and while the sun rose higher the long arguments flew back and forth. Mike and I kept silent, since anything else seemed a waste of effort, and besides, our Persian vocabulary did not measure up to the occasion. Nevertheless, by midday we appeared to be winning our case, for the unfortunate mule driver had several counts against him: he was from a rival village; he had a reputation as a troublemaker; and, to clinch the argument, he had already been going up the valley with his mules when he met us. Under these circumstances it was deemed an act of charity to pay him anything at all for his miserable beasts. With profuse apologies for the muleteer's behavior the headman told us that we owed nothing and then sent his own nephew to guide us to the castle of Hasan ibn-al-Sabbah.

The Eagle's Nest is built on the flat crown of the Rock of Alamut, a vast sandstone bolder that juts out from the side of the deep valley. To reach the top of the rock one climbs a narrow footpath that curls around into the gap between the rock and the mountain behind it. There, in the shadows, one has a few moments of tricky footwork on the loose, crumbling surface of the trail before stepping out onto the crown of the rock to take in the view that the Grand Master must once have enjoyed. The only horizon is the long gray line of mountain peaks, half shrouded in clouds and appearing to hang in space. Far below, the cloud shadows chase each other across paddy fields divided by the glint of sunlight on streamlets, and from one end of the valley to the other there are the little groves of trees that surround the toy-like Assassin villages.

Today there is very little left of Hasan's fortress on top of the rock—only a few rather disappointing stumps of stone walls and a couple of caverns in which, it is said, the Assassins stored honey and grain that never spoiled during the one hundred and sixty-six years of their rule of the Alamut. Seven Grand Masters followed Hasan ibn-al-Sabbah, but they failed to match the founder's genius. Gradually the power of the Assassins ebbed away.

The end came in 1256; yet, in a sense, the *fida'i* were not disgraced since they were defeated by one of the most ruthless military machines of all

Explorers of the Assassins' lair, the author, center, and Michael de Larrabeiti, right, rejoin a third colleague, after following Marco Polo's steps.

time—the Mongol army under Hulagu Khan. The Assassins were forewarned that the Mongols had decided to crush them, and they appealed to the Christian princes to come to their aid against a common foe. But Europe was only too pleased that the Assassins had at last met their match and, in the words of the Bishop of Winchester, sent back the cold reply "Let Dog eat Dog."

So Hulagu came with his squadrons of mounted archers, his Iranian auxiliaries, and his Chinese engineers skilled in siege warfare and equipped with mangonels and giant crossbows capable of hurling a javelin more than twenty-five hundred paces. The Alamut could, perhaps, have held out; there were tanks of food and ample supplies of weapons, and water was piped to the Eagle's Nest through channels hewn into the solid rock. But the heart had gone out of the Nizaris. Their last Grand Master, Kwur Shah, vacillated. His councilors advised him to sue for peace, and so Kwur Shah left the Alamut to surrender himself to Hulagu. For three days the inhabitants of the rock were allowed to carry away their possessions, and then Mongol troops moved in to pull down the walls and demolish all standing fortifica-

tions. Several of the other Assassin castles put up a fight, but without the Alamut and their Grand Master it was hopeless. Kwur Shah was eventually executed by the Mongols and thousands upon thousands of Nizaris were systematically rounded up and put to death. The power of the Assassins was snuffed out; in the words of the Arab historian Juvaini: "Of him [the last Grand Master] and his stock no trace was left, and he and his kindred became but a tale on men's lips and a tradition in the world."

But history was to prove Juvaini wrong. At the end of the fifteenth century there was a Nizari revival, and a new imam came forward. Much later, in the nineteenth century, the reigning imam fled from Iran to India for political reasons, and the large overseas community of Nizari Ismailians accepted him as their leader. His heir, of the same name, and spiritual descendant of the Lords of Alamut, is the present Aga Khan.

Although Timothy Severin is just twenty-seven and has only recently finished his graduate work at Oxford, he has already written two full-scale histories of travel—one on the exploration of the Mississippi and the other on Marco Polo.

Hegel, Hegel, the Gang's All Ears By GORDON COTLER

Our time is a time for crossing barriers, for erasing old categories—for probing around. When two seemingly disparate elements are imaginatively poised, put in apposition in new . . . ways, startling discoveries often result.

Learning, the educational process, has long been associated only with the glum. We speak of the "serious" student. Our time presents a unique opportunity for learning by means of humor—a perceptive or incisive joke can be more meaningful than platitudes lying between two covers. "The Medium Is the Massage" is a . . . collide-oscope of interfaced situations.

—Marshall McLuhan,
The Medium Is the Massage

JANUARY 4: Urtigan continues to be a spiritual pollutant in the atmosphere of Philosophy Hall. This morning he pinned me to the corridor wall as I emerged from my 11 o'clock to urge that I attend what he called a "Faculty Freedom" rally tonight. When I told him I have never felt more free to speak my mind than right here on this campus, he said, "I sing of freedom from *want*, Baby," and rubbed thumb against forefinger like a stock-company Shylock. That man's very existence diminishes our profession. He certainly extinguished the little glow with which I had left Room 414, a glow occasioned by my having just delivered, with perhaps even more startling clarity than last year, my increasingly popular lecture on Spinoza's crisis of ethic. For fifty minutes, not so much as a shoulder had twitched among these ordinarily spastic undergraduates, and afterward, as I was putting on my rubbers, young Bootlyk, a bright and sensitive student I've noticed before, shuffled up diffidently and somewhat wet-eyed to mumble that he had always expected, on graduation, to join his father in the family cat-food business, but that this semester of Philosophy 203 had shaken his values sufficiently so that he was now planning a life of contemplation, probably with the Trappists in the hills of Tennessee. It is precisely such nuggets of psychic reward that make this calling worthwhile, and when Urtigan comes whining in my ear about cost-of-living adjustments, or to compare my salary scale with that of a septic tank

repairman, I could punch his loutish face.

Tried twice this afternoon to see Stentorios about my teaching schedule for next year—a lighter load would give me needed time to finish the new book—but was unable on either occasion to secure his attention. At two o'clock he had a portable television on his desk and was absorbed in a program called—I'm almost certain I have this right—"My Little Margie." He seemed slightly embarrassed, and waved me out of his office with a remark about a periodic need to clear his head of "linear thinking patterns." At four o'clock, when I returned, he was buried in the new McLuhan book, moving his lips ever so slightly, and would not be disturbed. A department chairman who has no time for his staff ought to stand down, but Stentorios thinks the job is his by birthright because his father was a *paisano* of Aristotle.

* * *

JANUARY 8: Was so unnerved during my 11 o'clock by the whooping and braying that issued from the adjoining classroom (Urtigan's, naturally) that I was obliged to knock back a full half-ounce shot of sherry to steady myself for lunch. I am certain that Urtigan has set out deliberately to irritate me because I would not join his wretched pay-raise movement, but I have not yet learned how he gets his students—almost on cue, it seems—to set up that dreadful seal-like barking and yowping. Driven past the point of patience (and perhaps somewhat emboldened by the sherry), I stormed into Stentorios's office this afternoon to register a complaint, forcing him to switch off his television. Before I had completed my introductory remarks, in which Urtigan's name figured unflatteringly, Stentorios held up a hand to silence me, and then did something utterly weird. He turned himself upside down in his chair to balance on the back of his neck and began to pull off his shirt and tie. As I stood in open-mouthed astonishment, he shouted, "Don't

knock Urtigan! This department must learn to take off in new directions!" I fled.

* * *

FEBRUARY 1: I think I have an explanation for Stentorios's seeming madness of yesterday. Despite my upset, which was only partly alleviated by my soaking in a hot tub for an hour last night, I lectured not too badly today. I was leaving my 2 o'clock, after flooding with a clear, steady light Kierkegaard's crisis of ethic, when Ravigotte, the Frenchman in our department, pulled me into a corner of the corridor, obviously dying to impart some morsel of campus gossip. I told him I had no time to talk, as I was on my way to the library for some digging on my book, but he said, "Forget the book. The guidon of the Philosophy Department now reads, 'Pun or perish.'" He explained that Stentorios was taking department members aside one at a time to lay down an ultimatum for more humor in their classes. "You're all too effete," Ravigotte quoted him as saying. "No philosopher has any more to say to today's youth than a good salty joke." And then (Ravigotte swore), he added, "So don't put Descartes before the coarse." Before the poor Frenchman could stumble blindly from his office, Stentorios had extracted a promise from him to call the Socratic dialogues he conducts at home afternoons with his students, "*Sacré* Teas."

The nature of the strange laughterlike sounds issuing from Urtigan's classes is now clear: it is laughter. I have not heard a word from him about faculty salaries for at least a week, and I will bet my morocco-bound set of Maimonides against a paperback volume of Sartre that as reward for his japery the fool has been quietly promised the full professorship that opens up next year. We shall see about that: Stentorios has asked for a conference with me tomorrow, and I will ascertain once and for all which it is that counts on this campus, scholarship or good-fellowship.

* * *

FEBRUARY 2: What a day! I have poured myself a liberal Cherry Heering to give me the

DRAWINGS BY CHARMATZ

strength to record it. First, to confirm my suspicions about Urtigan's antics sufficiently to confront Stentorios with them, I found an excuse to slip out of my 11 o'clock for a minute about halfway through the hour, leaving the class to peel several layers of meaning from my exegesis of Hume's crisis of ethic. Edging up to the door of Urtigan's classroom, I waited for the inevitable burst of braying laughter that comes at intervals never longer than three minutes, and opened the door a crack. My worst fears were confirmed. Urtigan, perched on his desk with his legs crossed, and strumming the window pole as though it was a bass fiddle, was crooning into the simpering face of a coed:

"I Kant give you anything but pu-ure reason, That's Manny's line for the seventeen-eighty wo-one season . . ."

I shut the door and returned at once to my own class. Need I add that I took up with enthusiasm Hume's argument that knowledge is limited to phenomena experienced?

Fortified by almost half a bottle of India Pale Ale, I presented myself at the appointed hour at Stentorios's office, prepared to battle fiercely for the principle that, in teaching, substance is all. When I entered, Stentorios clicked a wall switch that threw the room into total darkness (he had drawn the drapes before my arrival) and said, "Sit down, Werbler." After I had soundly cracked my shins and elbows, he observed, "There's our Philosophy Department in a nutshell—stumbling in the dark, eager to have the way lighted." With that he flicked on an usher's flashlight and beamed it at a pyramid of books on top of the wardrobe. They were all copies of McLuhan's *The Medium Is the Massage*. "Take one. Read it. Apply it," he said, "or it's *there* for you." And now the flashlight featured his wastebasket. "Your classes, Werbler," he concluded, "are positively funereal."

The light winked out and the room was filled with the sound of "The Dead March" from *Saul*. Over it I shouted all my objections to this kind of rot. I was well prepared to speak my piece, and the anger that was building in me made me perhaps more eloquent than I would have been had my adrenalin not been pumping. I said all the right things, and I said them before "The Dead March" had built up to its climax. *I* provided the climax: in my peroration I made it clear that I was taking the matter directly to the president of the university. A moment later the room lights popped on. Stentorios was nowhere to be seen, but a new element had been added to the scene. A paper panel about five feet high and two across, framed in wood, now stood in front of the wardrobe, from which it had certainly been removed. Filling the panel was a stenciled reproduction of a frankfurter roll. About the time I had made up my mind that Stentorios was lurking behind it, he burst through the paper, reeking of ouzo, and said confidentially, "Werbler, I'd like to step out of my role and give you some man-to-man advice. Don't buck this thing. It's President Baldwin himself who is pressing for it." Saying the name seemed to open some floodgate that had kept his emotions in check. He collapsed trembling into his chair, on the edge of tears, and blurted out a story of massive pressure on him from the university administration either to brighten up the department's pedagogical approach—or retire.

"B-Baldwin called me to his office," he sobbed, "and lectured me on an anticipated drop in the rise in our admission-applications curve. He-he had an electric toaster on his desk. After he'd talked a minute, up popped two paper-bound copies of *The Medium Is the Massage*. He-he said, 'This is a red-hot book. Get with it or get out.' " Stentorios's face went hard. "And I say the same to you, Werbler. Do you swing with the department, or is this where you get off?"

When I left him, a wreck of a man pasting a fresh hot-dog roll poster into the wooden frame, my heart went out to him. He is too old to make a fresh start. But I'm not. This very night I begin discreetly hinting to certain universities of my availability.

With my not inconsiderable name in the field, a generous selection of positions will be open to me.

* * *

APRIL 18: A deeply rewarding day of lecturing, with teacher-student rapport as subtle as the interplay among the instruments of the Budapest String Quartet. It is days like this that make one proud of one's calling—and of the caliber of students at this splendid institution! Even if one of the schools that could not, at present, find a place for me on its faculty should eventually discover an opening, wild horses could not drag me from the stimulating atmosphere of this campus. My 9 o'clock class, for example, was one appreciative chuckle from first bell to last. But the high point of my day was the sight of Urtigan's anxious face poking through the door in the middle of my 11 o'clock to ask if we would keep down the volume of laughter to a level at which he could conduct his class. I was using some of my new Nietzsche material, and it does lean a bit more to the boff than the giggle. At the end of the hour a brilliant young student named Bootlyk, whose development I've been watching with delight, came up with eyes wet with laughter and shining with admiration as I was putting away my props, to observe that he had always planned to go into the family publishing business on graduation, but that this semester of Philosophy 203 had shaken his convictions to their foundations, and that, thanks to me, he was now headed for a career as a media man in advertising. It is the opportunity we are given to shape young lives that makes life at this university more than merely status-factory!

Gordon Cotler writes novels, short stories, and (under a pseudonym) mysteries. Two of his books have been made into movies. This spoof is his first contribution to HORIZON.

ROME DIDN'T FALL IN A DAY

By MIKE THALER

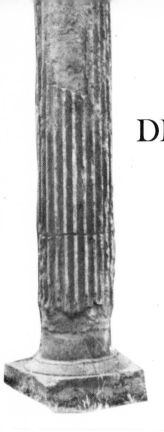

This used to be such a nice drive

This neighborhood certainly has gone down

The younger generation just has no respect for other people's property

Happy birthday, Junior

So eat!

Where did we fail him?